STORM STILL

THE GERMAN LIST

PETER HANDKE

STORM STILL

TRANSLATED BY
MARTIN CHALMERS

LONDON NEW YORK CALCUTTA

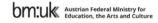

This publication was supported by a grant from the Goethe-Institut India and
by the Austrian Federal Ministry of Education, Arts and Culture

Seagull Books, 2018

Peter Handke, *Immer noch Sturm*
© Suhrkamp Verlag, 2010

English translation © Martin Chalmers, 2014

First published in English translation by Seagull Books, 2014

ISBN   978 0 8574 2 558 4

British Library Cataloguing-in-Publication Data
A catalogue record for this book is available from the British Library

Typeset by Seagull Books, Calcutta, India
Printed and bound by Maple Press, York, Pennsylvania, USA

Amère ironie de pretendre persuader et convaincre, alors
que ma certitude profonde est que la part du monde encore
susceptible de rachat n'appartient qu'aux enfants,
aux héros et aux martyrs.

Georges Bernanos
Les grands cimetières sous la lune

Bitter irony—to imagine that it is possible to persuade and to
convince, whereas I am as certain as can be, that the part of the
world still accessible to salvation belongs to the children,
the heroes and the martyrs alone.

Georges Bernanos
A Diary of My Times

'I'
My mother
My grandparents
Gregor, 'Jonatan', *my mother's oldest brother*
Valentin, *the second oldest brother*
Ursula, 'Snežena', *my mother's sister*
Benjamin, *the youngest brother*

one

A heath, steppe, a steppe-like heath, or wherever. Now, in the Middle Ages, or whenever. What can be seen there? In the middle distance, a bench, of no particular period, and beside or behind it or somewhere an apple tree, laden with about ninety-nine apples, early apples, almost white, or late apples, dark red. This heath appears to slope gently, it's homely. To whom does it show itself? To whom does it appear like this? To me, here, at this moment. I saw it in bygone times, in another time, and see it again now, together with the bench, on which I once sat with my mother, on a warm, still summer or autumn afternoon, I think, far from the village, and yet close to home. Uncommonly wide was and is that homeland horizon. Whether memory deceives or not—from far off angeluson one side, then far off on the other, the ringing of the Angelus bell. And even if this is again an illusion—in retrospect, it seems that my mother and I are holding hands. And altogether there in my memory everything is happening in pairs; the birds in the sky are flying in pairs, the butterflies are fluttering in pairs through the air, the dragonflies are whirring in pairs and so on. It's true, I encountered the little apple tree, with its luminescent apples, one way or another, at yet another time, in a night-time moment, in a daydream, or whenever. At first I sat there with my eyes shut. Now I open them. And what do I see then? My forebears are approaching from every side, with the typical Jaunfeld gait, one foot firmly following the other. Each one comes along alone, except my grandparents as a couple, alone the more or less or perhaps not at all deranged sister of my mother, and likewise, walking alone, their three brothers each on a separate path or not-path. The youngest is doing somersaults rather, rolling along, as if in high spirits. Each one makes for the place to stand that seems prescribed for them, again apart from my grandparents, who sit on the bench. This couple is not old at all, and their five children are without exception young, even the first born, the one-eyed brother there with the thick moustache, born, after all, quite long before the others. The youngest of the sons is still almost a child, and my mother appears to me literally blossom-young and almost like the secret lover of the middle brother, already known early on and far and wide as a ladies' man. (Her hardly older sister, on the other hand, was supposedly never 'blossom-young'.) And, just so I don't forget—they all appear to me in black and white, not only their garments, and all of them beautiful, as people always are in black and white. Strange that these figures do not at all resemble my forebears as they are impressed on my memory from life or from photographs or from stories. They do not, not in appearance, nor posture, nor expressions. And at the same time it is them. It is them! And it fits with that, that they now discover me in my place and, startled, delighted, irritated, indifferent, quiet, loud, recognize me, one after the other. There rises a many-voiced 'Hello! Fancy that. Good Lord. So it's him. You're here!' followed, as with one voice, by the chorus of sighs familiar in our family and clan and then with one voice or ten, 'Come on, latecomer. Jump onto the family train, Descendant. The only one who still dreams us. Oh, if only someone else would dream us for once! Someone more disinterested. Someone who thinks and reflects on us—and not your eternal commemoration, your perpetual evocation. In a word, a third party! Can't you finally leave us in peace? But now that you're here, last in line, this way, come into the picture with us.'

I had to be told at least three times before I complied with the invitation, or the command, or whatever it was. I hesitated, as is my way. Having stood up, I sat down again. Halfway there, on the threshold of the steppe-like heath, I wanted to turn on my heel. And finally, having reached my ancestors, I wanted to hide behind one of them; not behind my grandparents, and not behind my mother's apron strings—she was indeed wearing an apron, one for holidays, such as in another time the village women wore—and not behind the biggest and oldest of the brothers. But? Behind the youngest and smallest. Like that I must have become even more visible—a present-day commonplace figure, one of millions, in the appropriate intercontinental dress, already at first sight in contrast to the timeless rural Sunday-best garments of my forebears. Also conspicuous about me, again in contrast to the others, is that I appear as someone already advanced in years, older even than my grandparents. Going by my age, I could, for example, be the fairly elderly 'father' of my 'blossom-young' mother.

Her youngest brother, the almost-child, with me in his shadow, stepped to the side again and again, three times, let's say, and I moved with him. And at the same time the clan, led by my mother, has likewise come closer and formed a loose semicircle round me. This joint movement did not disturb me, however—I finally came up to my people and gave each of them in turn my hand (any other form of touching was, or is, hardly ever considered by our kind). Only in front of my mother did I pause, keeping a little distance, and said: 'Here you are, forebears. I have waited for you for a long time. It is not I who do not leave you in peace. It doesn't leave me in peace, let me rest. You don't leave me in peace, not ever. Hello, Mother! Haven't set eyes on you for ages. And you still talk with an accent foreign to this part of the world, as if Napoleon's troops were still the masters of Carinthia and Carniola, you French-woman of the Karawank Mountains. Good day, Grandmother, stara mati, dober dan. Good day, Grandfather, stari oče, dober dan, tesar, or carpenter. Good day, Uncle and Godfather Gregor, moj stric in moj boter, my uncle and my godfather, dober dan. Good day, Teta, that is, Aunt, Ursula, no fear, and least of all here, of me. Hello there, Mother-brother Valentin, English speaker of our fam-ily, chess master, also otherwise a small master. Good day and dober dan, stric Benjamin, you almost-child, for whom the earth of the tundra, in accordance with the inscription on the memorial stone, should be light. And now you, Mother—you were never as young as now in my day and night eyes. And now you are also a different figure, with different features, a different voice, a different accent, your eyes a different colour. And yet you are the same. It's you. But, tell me: Where have we all come together now? Because this doesn't appear to be our district, apart, perhaps, from the apple tree there. Except back home the apples look quite different, that is, like apples good enough to bite into, to steal. And the shrivelled stuff there tempts one neither to take a bite nor to become an apple thief, and not at all to commit a sin. (Stealing fruit was never a sin in our district—or is it one meanwhile?) And our district and this terrain here—there's no comparison. What is that-there supposed to represent? A heath? The steppe? The taiga? The tundra? As for me—it makes me want to run away. Except that the next terrain is fairly certainly a degree more godforsaken and the stop after that quite certainly a cesspit and the one after that as sure as fate a minefield and so on, until at last there's no place at all.' My blossom-young mother replied immediately: 'I, too, did not recognize you at first. And before you began to speak, I was—uncertain. But now I know, it's you, my son. My son, who will never belong to us here, to the family, to the clan, fatherless, looking for a substitute, support and light with your forebears. And now to your question, which yet again was none at all. Yes, this here is our district. It's the Jaunfeld, in the land of Carinthia, Koroška in Slovene, lepa Koroška, beautiful Carinthia. And back *there* somewhere you must or can imagine our Saualpe Mountains or the Svinjska planina, which, although from a distance lie there like a giant sow or swine, in reality take their name from the lead, in our home language called svinec, the lead or svinec inside the mountains, from which come . . . come . . . help me, Son, no, don't help me, there issue, stem the wild summer thunderstorms on the Svinjska planina or Saualpe, and likewise our home and family name, remember, no, don't remember, you've always had a bad memory, take note, my son. And take note—for us here, to have pig luck means to be lucky, and to walk on the Saualpe means for us to walk with a spring in one's step, to walk without leaden feet.'

I briefly played along with her game as she had done with mine before: 'And what do I have to imagine back *there*? A cudgel mountain, a vale of tears, a devil's glen, a dragon wall, a stony sea, a mammoth fart gorge, a suicide ridge?'

My mother stopped playing my game. 'Back there you can imagine the Karawank Alps, and then behind them Slovenia, Yugoslavia.'

I, in an attempt to go on with the game: 'But Jugoslavija hasn't existed for ages, not the royal one after the First World War and certainly not the one without a king after the Second. Which time applies here anyway? When is now? The time of heath and steppe, or what? Sunday-apron time? Knickerbocker time? Butter-churn time? Apple-grafting time? Dung-spreading time? Maize-, or what was the phrase again, Turk-stripping time, when you all squatted in the barn in the evening, peeling maize and pretending it was another time as you told stories and sang songs? Or the real time after all, historical time, the shitty time, lost for ever, lost by you and by me, and you worriers, we worriers, lead-heavily lost in it?'

Thereupon my girl-mother: 'Unfamiliar figure, familiar language. By your language I recognize you, Monkey-Son. All of us gathered here can be recognized by our language, at least we recognize one another, each of us can recognize another as one of us. No one in the district spoke as we did. No one in the whole land speaks as we do, will have spoken as we did. Show him.'

A general pause. The first to speak then is the mother-brother, whom I addressed as 'Valentin'. (As he steps forward I see that he really is wearing something like 'knickerbockers'.): 'I, the only son who survived the war, the only one who became little bit wealthy and, well, powerful, owe it above all to the fact that I broke away from our accursed home and clan language. Yes, damn this language, which robbed Benjamin and Gregor there of their lives, the one in furthest Russia, the other right here on the accursed, leaden Saualpe, broke our mother's heart, pushed our father's hat down over his eyes, his ears and then over his mouth, too, with the sweatband as self-imposed gag, the language which cost my sister Ursula her dearest, her only, her bridegroom, even before love could be put into words, never mind become affectionate—the man only, what's the word, "bridegroomed", you bridegroomed, the two of you, didn't you, for years, until your language did you part, your bridegroom was off—groomed off—and you remained alone, Sister, with your language, your substitute bridegroom.' (If I heard rightly, she interjected, 'No, the true one!') 'And let it be damned, our language'—he had abruptly turned to me—'which spoken by her, my favourite sister here, or, if you like, your, well, why not, Mother, it's not her fault, woman is woman, let it be damned, our language, which, spoken by my darling, my darling Clementine, awakened desire in the ears not only of the men of the village but also of all the homeland associations, so that each one who heard, how she, she in particular, spoke our language, wanted her, her over there, wanted her on the spot. Strange, by the way, how a certain language and a certain way of speaking it can get one going, didn't I experience it for myself, when I was off duty in Narvik and heard the Lapp woman talking, not to me at all, in the distance, at the other end of the street, and at the same moment here by my ribs, so that it literally trickled over me—except that the one who then took my sweetheart home or snapped her up, was your father—I need say no more about that—and like father, like son, there's nothing more to be said about it.'

Again a general pause. After that my grandparents sat down on the bench on the steppe-like heath or on the 'Jaunfeld', with their adolescent youngest son between them. And then the sombre, also sombrely dressed, young woman whom I addressed as my mother's elder sister, called 'Ursula', had her say: 'You were all against me, from when I was little. I never found my place with you. You never let me play with you in any game. And if you did, then you had a good laugh at me at the first opportunity. You especially, Sister—oh, how you could make fun of me. Everything died in me at your laughter, died, everything. And when I locked myself into the lavatory outside, you went on laughing at the door, the one with the heart. Heartless, heartless. So I ran away from you all into the forest, but the forest, particularly our dark spruce forest, never did me any good. On my return I was as dark as it is, in your eyes I was the spoilsport. And yet for a long time I believed in happiness, in my happiness, and could imagine nothing finer than to be playing, with you, with my family. Only all the parts were taken, and to sit there silently, like our mother, was out of the question for me. I wanted to be in the thick of things and to pitch in, yes, pitch in. But why on earth? That was how it was meant to be, yes, that was what was meant to be. As a result I probably did wither away into the person you had seen me as being ever since I was little, into the person who in our district is called "single and displeased", someone who lets others feel that she isn't loved. It's true, no one has ever loved me, not even my mother. From the moment of my birth she only pitied me. But what use is pity to me? I spit on it. Pity and your laughter chased me out of the house as soon as I left school, and until the war I lived as one for whom there was no place in the house, as a maid among strangers, as was usual then for us who were away from home. And in the middle of the peace, which you all found so heavenly, isn't it so, Gregor, you fruit farmer, so biblical, my thoughts had already long been in the war. In the war, so I thought, I will at last find my place. In the war I will be loved. And is that what happened? If I only knew. In the house, for sure, from one day to the next, there were three places free, and I was made welcome, lovingly, as it seemed to me, even by you, Sister. But . . . but . . . earlier my place had been with the cows and the horses in the byre and the stable more than anywhere else, or in your orchard, Gregor, occasionally. But now—nowhere any more. So perhaps it's true, after all, the other saying from our district, "Only he finds a place who brings it with him"? Did I perhaps never, how can I put it, embody having a place? And perhaps that's exactly why I became the spoilsport for you, worse, the cause of misfortune? It was not you, then, who didn't leave a place for me, rather that I was already born placeless, and hence wanted nothing less than war, world war or family war? Pity, Mother. Did you not tell me that in our language here "womb" and "pity" have the same root?'

Already during this tirade, no doubt familiar in the family, my grandmother, until then sitting completely still next to her husband and 'Benjamin' on the bench on the heath, awkwardly and rather noisily fished her knitting things, wool and knitting needles, out of her best bag, or whatever it is, and prepared to go on knitting a sock, or whatever, that she had already started. As a countermove her husband, my grandfather, took a tightly folded, chequered, 'good' handkerchief out of the inside pocket of his Sunday-best jacket and just as awkwardly unfolded it until it was resplendent in its almost dishcloth size, and blown his nose into it. Following that, with all of us round him, he related one of his short stories, familiar in the family: 'Long before I met your mother, long before the First World War, I was once locked up for a couple of hours by the gendarmes, in the local gaol, that is, in the cell next to the police station, no, not for resisting an officer going about his duty, which is what we are otherwise known for—I'm afraid I must disappoint you there. But this is what happened. I had finished my apprenticeship as a carpenter, but when it came to women—nothing, nothing at all. I didn't have the bottle to approach anyone, which is indeed another trait of our clan, with certain exceptions, but then very decided ones, take Valentin there, our vigorous son, the name reveals the man, notorious beyond the community boundaries and beyond the Jaunfeld here throughout the whole Carinthian basin as—does one still use the word?—a womanizer, who—it's not what we said then—didn't miss any opportunity and didn't let any bed go cold, except his own . . . Anyway, how to find a woman, me, me! at last? I hardly spoke any German then, like almost everyone from the country here. School? Absent—excused, not excused. The first person to teach me a bit of German was a tramping carpenter, from Bremen or Hamburg or Eckernförde or whatever those dumps up in the north are called, and our girls ran after him and ran into his arms, didn't they. But why? There were those of us who said because of his special carpenter's clothes, his broad-brimmed hat and moleskin trousers, behind which the girlies didn't expect Johnny Cash or Graham Nash, but infatuated with operettas as they were—that's the way it still was back then—a tsar in disguise, or at least one of his sailors. And the others, because he spoke German. Did not one of these German speakers turn your mother's Slav head, mon petit fils, moj vnuk, mu engene, mi nieto? Until well into the Second World War in our district, speaking proper German didn't just open the front doors and the yard gates. Anyone speaking nothing but German held the promise of being a gentleman. German, in those days was the magnetic pole for the females here. But how did it come about that your father was locked up in the cell that time? It was a Wednesday—I don't know why I bother you with the day of the week—it was market day in Völkermarkt, Bleiburg or wherever. And I was arrested because at one particular stand I bought cow's eyes, a whole bucketful, which was on offer there, to make beef soup, that's the way it was, and because then, from one end of the town to the other, I threw some of these eyes, they were really slippery, not a few slipped out of my hand, at young women, also at a few who were not so young—and in fact I didn't even throw the eyes, still less bombard the girls, rather I threw the eyes to them—they were intended for them, gently, almost like roses, and, like roses, without thorns, innocent. And I really was innocent. Because what had the German carpenter advised me to do about my woman problem?'

Here the sombre one of his two daughters finally interrupted the storyteller: 'Father, you've already told us the story a thousand and one times, except that the one throwing the eyes was always someone else, the village idiot, the clod from next door or whoever. Father, why have you always wanted to divert attention? Why can't you be serious for once? Have not almost all of us ultimately got lost, not only us, but also our whole people? Penultimate act—general jubilation, last act—the great fall, without even a whimper. If our history is not a tragedy—what else is it?—'

Here she is interrupted in turn by her father. He has jumped up from the bench. And he talks loudly, he almost shouts, then even roars for a moment: '"Tragedy": I don't ever want to hear the word! I'd rather hear the stupidest other foreign words than that—"Bugs Bunny", "lumberjack", "confiture", "etagère", "quark", "petit pois", "torte", "pumpernickel" . . . There's no place for a tragedy in our house and no place for a tragic actress. So don't complain that you never found your place here, you requiem addict. We want no professional mourners here! No greater contradiction than that, between our people and tragedy. A "tragedy"? I don't know the word. At the first hint of tragedy—switched off in an instant. Our innermost being, it resists the tragic, resists tragic behaviour, tragic demeanour. Our songs are often sad? Yes, all too often, and so sad that I've had it up to my neck, that they go in one ear and out the other, that just the first whining note makes me want to pee. Our people often calls itself, all too often, People of Suffering? Yes, but suffering and enduring are not tragic! The passive, the traditional, dearly beloved, celebrated form of suffering—what's tragic about it? Our history has done without tragedies. Tragedy presumes— having become active, becoming active, one way or another. And our nature has always been anti-tragic and, accordingly, with time against action.' (Is he not gradually becoming confused, evident also in his voice growing quieter?) 'Or has our nature always been against collective action, and, accordingly, has it with time become anti-tragic? Has our nature accordingly determined our history? Or, on the contrary, has our history determined our nature? Our history of suffering: Does it come from our passive nature? Or does our passive nature come from our history of suffering? And did we not once after all become active, active as no other people far and wide in the middle of Europe?' (Abruptly he becomes vehement again.) 'It's the word! The word really gets on my wick! Tragic, tragedy. Alchemy. Balcony. Tapestry. Philately. "Washbasin" instead of our "lavoir". "China cupboard" instead of "sideboard". "Jacket" instead of "coat". And the names! Kai! Jürgen! Uwe! Thorsten! Gunter . . . Gernot . . . Giselher . . . With your alien lan- guage you've profaned the holy air of our homeland. Tragedy— that word won't come through my door! Glory! Just one German word from the Reich made me sit up and take notice—"Bleibe". Bleibe—a place to stay!—instead of the same old song about

"Heimat"—homeland—and "domovina"!' He sits down again, fishes the pocket watch out of the pocket of his Sunday-best waistcoat and winds it up. He holds it to his ear. The general pause.

And then once again my grandfather: 'Whoever says "sideboard" instead of "cupboard", "jacket" instead of "coat" and "brew" instead of "coffee" has already lost his homeland. He has already betrayed his homeland. And anyone who uses words like "brambles" and "russet apple" will never be a hangman. What I am, what we are, starts from a home, a house, from our house, and without a house we are nothing.'

And what do I see now? The oldest of the siblings, the one-eyed one, whom at the beginning I called 'Gregor', steps forward with his Jaunfeld gait, which with him resembles a dance, and proclaims, or, in the manner of the clan, plays the part of the proclaimer: 'After the Gloria, the solemn reading from the holy book of the family.' (He shows us this book, very large, rather slim, wrapped in packing paper marked by age.) 'My workbook, famous far and wide, on fruit-growing, titled *Sadjarstvo!*, that is, fruit science, with an exclamation mark!, Or, simply, fruit-growing, a record kept by me, Gregor Svinec or Gregor Bleier—as our name, as you know, was forcibly Germanized—from winter and spring nineteen thirty-six, the best time of my life, which I spent, as you all know, or don't know, on the other side of the state border, in Maribor pod Dravom, in German Marburg an der Drau, in the then first Yugoslavia, the royal one, in the agricultural college there or somewhere, no, exactly there, right there. And I'll now open the book for you, at random. Before that, however, I'll press my lips to it and smell it.' (He does so and then turns to me again.) 'Do as I have done,

Godson, and then pass the book round.' (Said, done—each of us kisses the book and sniffs at it in his or her own way; only the sombre sister refuses to take it. The book, back in the author's hands, is then opened as announced.) 'Jabolko Welschbrunner: Plod debel, pravilno oblaste oblike.' (He pauses, with a glance at my blossomyoung mother, at which she steps forward and translates.) 'The Welschbrunner apple: Thick fruit, as a rule rounded in shape.' (Her brother continues the reading.) 'Koža gladka, zelena, pozneje rumena na sončni strani živordeče barvana.' My mother translates: 'The skin green and smooth, later yellow, a lively red colouring on the sunny side.' The one-eyed brother: 'Na drevesu zori v prvi polovici oktobra in počaka do vigredi.' My mother, his sister: 'On the tree it ripens in the first half of October and keeps until spring.' (Gradually, the others have joined in the reading and translation, apart from, see above, and my grandmother who only moves her lips silently. Does she perhaps have a non-speaking part? Instead, she powerfully supports the rhythm with her knitting things.) The one-eyed: 'Drevo raste zelo močno in daje nato redne in bogate pridelke.' Almost all: 'The tree grows very strongly and then yields regular and abundant crops.' The one-eyed: 'Uspeva v vsaki zemlji in legi.' Almost all: 'It flourishes in every soil and environment . . .' Here the darker of the sisters intervenes: 'Lega means "location"! Not "environment"! "Location" and "environment" are not the same thing!' The one-eyed: 'Jabolko Welschbrunner je zelo pripravno za izdelavo sadnih sokov—' Almost all: 'The Welschbrunner Apple. It is particularly suitable for the production of fruit juices—' The dark sister: 'Of "fruit juices"!—the phrase "fruit juice" didn't exist then!' The one-eyed: 'Jabolko Welschbrunner je zelo pripravno za izdelavo sadnih sokov, ker ima mnogo kisline.' All (except me): 'The Welschbrunner is particularly suitable for the production of fruit juices because it is very acidic.' The one-eyed: 'Maribor, devet in dvajesetega februara tisoč devetsto šeštintrideset.' All (except me): 'Marburg, twenty-seventh February, nineteen thirty-six.' And the reader has shut his codex, briefly kissed it and then stepped back to his place or wherever. And then once more the general pause.

At this point in my journey through time, or whatever it is, the youngest of the siblings, the one whom at the beginning I addressed as 'Benjamin', the almost-child, at last makes his presence felt as an individual. Still seated, there between his parents, his voice is unexpectedly heard: 'Can . . . can . . . can someone explain to me why pears sometimes have the shape of an apple but an apple never has the shape of a pear? And how can I tell whether there's a worm in the apple? And why after nine hundred and ninety-nine yellow corncobs there's suddenly a black one? And why do all the male members of our family, despite the nine shoehorns in the house, have shoes that are trodden down at the back? And who invented the shoehorn? And why, when shelling peas, is there always a single pea hidden at the back of the pod? And why do the lemon pips slip through my fingers every time I try to pick them up? And why do I lose a twig from the broom every time I sweep the yard? And why does the saucer stick to the cup again every time I drink a mouthful of coffee? And why am I so disgusted by milk skin in my mouth? And by milk altogether, even though, isn't it so, Mother, even as a four year-old I supposedly still followed you round the house and yard and meadow, with a stool in my hand, in order to suck in your mother's milk standing?' (Turning to me) 'Don't look at me with such a silly expression, Nephew! It's possible!' (Turning back to the circle) 'Why all this disgust in me, this constant disgust? A family sickness, or just my own? Disgust at the first light of dawn.

Disgust at the cowering cat. Disgust at my name—at having any name at all. Disgust at the hole between the ribs of the One who was crucified, caused by the Roman soldier's lance tip. Disgust at the sleeve of my Sunday-best jacket touching me here on the back of my hand. Disgust at the hairless bulge and crack between the legs of the neighbour's daughter I worshipped. Disgust at the election posters with the monsters who scrap with each other. Disgust at Christmas. Disgust at the timid, much loved dog, then wept over as a carcass. Disgust at the smell of wet chicken feathers. Disgust at foreign parts, disgust already at all the foreign paths after the triangular crossroads at the end of the village, disgust even at the neighbour's corridor, the neighbour's cowshed, the neighbour's garden trellis, on which the grapes are after all a little sweeter than ours at home. And even more intense disgust at the next village, and even more so at the next valley where the dialect is just a little bit different from ours—disgust, indescribable revulsion. And disgust, which could not be more intense, at the nearest town and so on from one town to the next in this country. Strange, admittedly, that my disgust each and every time stops short at the borders, even if I just think of them. The other land, no matter which—disgust unthinkable and I disgust-free. And like the disgust at the space, so a revulsion at time, or rather at the units of time, the hour, the week, the month, the year, the year above all and, possibly much worse still, at the minute, at the very word—mi-nut . . . And, strange again, that the disgust is hardly noticeable before daybreak and disappears completely before nightfall and becomes almost longing before Easter Monday, the day of the Resurrection, and even more so in the nights before Christmas, before the day of the Birth, and that I then long for a different reckoning of time, no, not 'reckoning' at all, disgust at every kind of "reckoning", at numbers altogether—that I long for a different time.

No more thou numbrest, reckonest no time,
Each step is infinite, each step sublime.

'Disgust at my never-ending longing. And disgust at my, at our never-ending homesickness. Homesick for the bench in front of the house, for the smokehouse smell in the pantry, for the smell of apples in the cellar, for being looked at by my mother, for the litanies of curses of my father, longer than the All Saints' Day litany in church ever was, and the longer the better, homesickness, accursed homesickness, for the one eye of my one-eyed eldest brother, for the bragging of the other brother fresh from his love nights, for the muttering and grouching of the sombre sister, homesickness, wretched homesickness for the singing of the bright sister—even if sometimes I would like to cover my ears, when she really and truly starts her singing. Homesickness, when I've hardly left the house, for home and farm and family. Wretched, repulsive, never-ending homesickness! Why on earth did you call me Benjamin? I have to be the youngest for ever. Why not Hans? Lukas? Absalom? My name, my prison. Absalom! Absalom!'

And again the general pause. Then a song, and I only slowly realized who had begun to sing: the previous speaker's sister, my blossom-young mother. Although her singing, as well as what she sang, was not as melancholy as I had feared, I at first involuntarily covered my ears, following the example of her little brother, from whom incidentally I seem to have inherited more than just the aversion to a certain kind of singing. Whether then in the course of events he and I took our hands away from our ears of our own accord or whether someone struck his down, at which I, too, . . . I can now, in the light of the present day, no longer remember. What I do recall—that we both, Benjamin and I, at least as the song began, appeared as the decided non-singers of our clan, as the stubborn ones. Strange that the verses of my blossom-young mother's song have stuck in my mind word for word:

'The year nineteen hundred and thirty-six was our happy year. It was a year of sun and snow. Sun and snow, and that really was the whole story, nothing more. You came home, Brother, from the other land and brought the other land home to me. Taught me pride in our language—sun and snow. Made an estate out of our cottage and a farmstead out of our chicken shit coop, and out of house and farm a property, conceived of house and farm and field as one thing, as a ground for us all—sun and snow.

'In the year nineteen hundred and thirty-six, a great misery came over the land here. The neighbour's wife wept before the empty wall of the pantry, the neighbour ground his last tooth stumps, the neighbour's children fed on May bugs, potato peels and bumble-bees. A folk of labourers on starvation wages, of workers without work, of freedmen without freedom, of voters without a vote, of the unpaid without number, of enemies within the most peaceful communities. And of the homeless from the Obdacher Sattel to Montafon, of the unsaddled from the Walhalla as far as Gralla, the old-established only in penal establishments, fisticuffs even at funerals, civil war all year long, long after the cold twelfth of February.

'The year nineteen hundred and thirty-six was our happy year. It was a year of sun and snow. But that's not the whole story. While one brother found land and language for us on the other side of the border, my second brother went with our father workday after workday from farmer to farmer, right across the Sau or Blei Alps, as an underage journeyman carpenter and Sunday after Sunday from widow's bed to widow's bed as Look-at-what-I can-do. And while the one brother hedged round the wasteland here with fruit trees and, listen, marked out freedom, listen, freedom for himself and for us for the first time in our history, my youngest brother, unsuspecting, allowed himself to be interned, so that in a grammar school, as it's called, he would be the first of us to cast an evil spell on our coarse culture, and what happened then? He promptly fled home, as fast as possible, home from Greek, home from Latin, home from German, just home to the farmyard to his pissing, farting, shitting beasts, as fast as possible home to the familiar dialect and to the sounds of the ancient land, untouched by any culture of the mind. To muck out the shed and the sty was then his pleasure, and to sit in the pitch-dark smokehouse and cock his eyes at the sausages then became for our youngest the substitute for the teats of his mother's breast. And now that was the whole story. Nineteen hundred and thirty-six—our happy year. A year of sun and snow'—Here she was interrupted by her gloomy-eyed sister—'And of woe and yet more woe. And throngs of flies, not only on the farm horse's eyes. That's how you lost that eye, Gregor, in your glorious year, isn't that so? And your girl left you that year, no couple any more, isn't that so? And no woman far and wide who eyed up our one-eyed after that year, no couple any more, ever, isn't that so? And the lightning bolt that struck the People's Wireless Receiver—no more music for the people. And the manure pit, in which you very nearly drowned—typical non-swimmer, tipičen neplavalec. And the avalanche from the roof that broke the neck of your favourite cow. And you? Uninsured, typical. A year of sun and snow, a year like any other, a year of manure, misfortune and woe.'

Was there a pause again at this point? It seems, to me at least, that the following voice came to me out of something like it, although to begin with it is again unclear who the speaker is. Ah, it is the one addressed, the one-eyed brother. It is he who replies: 'And yet it was our happy year, even if our only one. After that, there were only a few happy days, no, just one—that at least. And our happy year, it didn't only begin at the front door, which you had garlanded all together on my return from the fruit-growing school in Slovenia, and it did not end with it either. That was in midsummer, between Corpus Christi and Assumption Day, after the second mowing, when there are hardly any meadow flowers in bloom any more, and despite that, you all, you too, Sister, had still found flowers, Godknowswhere, and woven them into the door garland. The triumphal arch of our clan. Yes, my favourite cow, "And so soft to milk!", you said that yourself, word for word. And the house Most, the first pressing, apples and pears mixed, the tart Jacques Lebel with the sweet Duchesse d'Angoulême, named after the king's daughter from Angoulême in France, the Emperor Alexander Apple with the Louise Bonne d'Avranches, the green-skinned, white-fleshed Madeleine pear with the special bulbous dappled Cardinal. And then the November pig-slaughtering party, the pig silenced and scalded, the cut along its back and the white pork fat becoming visible, five-, six-fingers thick and with it the pot with sauerkraut put on the stove by Mother and her call, "Come, all of you!" and how all of us were greasy round the mouth and elsewhere, and how we also brought the neighbour something of the bounty—although soon there was no more of that, no one thought of his neighbour any more when there was a celebration in the house, and, anyway, soon there was nothing more to celebrate. A happy year as far as the next late spring, perhaps? Easter—that there would still always be Easter, perhaps? And that with the meal, as before at Easter, we could still say "blessing", and that "Heavenly" was not just another word. And then the first reaping. How at the crack of dawn on the way to the meadows each of us wanted to be first with the scythe, and how we—it hasn't happened, for a long time, we don't even say the word any more—how we rejoiced, no, shrieked with delight, and then sang as we worked: "Mrzla rosa, ojstra kosa, rada reže travnike"—translate that for your bastard child, Sister.' (Which my mother promptly obeys: 'Cold dew, sharp scythe likes to cut the meadows.') 'Where does that still happen, that someone rejoices? A shriek of delight? How devoutly everything was nevertheless performed that year on our properties. And how all that the heart desired was produced there at home. Did not you yourself, dark Sister, once call me King of Farmers?'

And how did the sister addressed reply? 'Never mind, One-Eye Farmer. And what you proclaimed there—the false gospel, the false good tidings. If I now cross myself—' (she does so) '—then not before God's name, God's Word. Performed the work devoutly? Don't make me laugh.' (She laughs with a joylessness, which in our family, and not just there, I remember only from her. Did she ever laugh at all?) 'For a while, during the year, we did all work together. But how you could curse then—with your cursing you even put our father in the shade, famous far and wide for his curses. You didn't just swear but cursed, cursed to Hell, damned to Hell—bloody sun, bloody rain, damned slope!—together with the wheat sheaves at the curve in the track where the wagon fell on its side—damn you and damn the horse and the bloody curve in the track and the whole godforsaken place! It was enough for an apple to fall on your head and you would threaten to uproot the whole tree. Couldn't get the boots off your feet and you wanted to smash the bootjack to pieces because of it. One of your grafts dried up and you damned it utterly and, beyond it, our local earth and air and so on, right up to the world and the universe as a whole. It's true, of course, that you were the most peaceable man in a thousand. But you could also be different, quite different and, later, during the war, you then proved that to the world. Work was sweet for you, that's true. But in the twinkling of an eye it could turn sour for you, your sweat sour instead of fine and salty, your blessed working-away suddenly ill-fated. And with your sudden veering from enthusiasm to curses you intimidated everyone round you. We were able to laugh at our father's curses, secretly at least, but when it came to your damnings I would have liked to hide away every time, I felt I was included in your cursing. You inspired me and you dumbfounded me, Brother mine. And so, in the year of thirty-six, when it became evident, that our produce, the property, the estate, the manor, your royal farm, were simply unable to feed us all, I even felt it right, to begin with at least, to have to leave home, to be among strangers, as a maid. And what bounty did we hundreds, we hecatombs of maids and labourers get to eat there? Main meal—dry bread crusts with boiling water poured over them. And what must did we drink? The first pressing? A joke. The second, in which the fruit mash is crushed once more, mixed with water—the diluted must? Another joke—it was for guests.' (Has she not long ago turned away from her brother to me or whoever, to a larger circle?) 'For us female and male hirelings, as we maids

and labourers are called, there is as drink the third pressing. A saving on waste and taste. And where do we sleep? Somewhere, in a
byre, somewhere in the byre. During the war then, with the partisans in the forest, at times I even longed for such a cow-warm shed.
And what do we have to wear? A garment of such stiff linen that
it is constantly biting into one's skin as if we had lice and, anyway,
we really do have lice. And what is the so holy work that we
hirelings do from one end of the holy homeland to the other? Col-
lecting the holy dew in little perfume bottles to be sent out over-
seas? No, now in the pre-war years, we at best cart the dung out
onto the fields, for the seed of the winter corn, and spread the
dung, pressed and pressed again by the beasts in the byre, first,
second and third pressings, the three-hundred-and-thirty-third
pressing, become so firm and heavy that we need a special pitch-
fork, an especially strong one, to spread it—and, listen! to evenly
distribute the holy dung! so that no unholy windows appear in the
rye and wheat field—the dung pitchforked apart, the hearts pitchforked up—holy, holy, holy!'

And once again her father jumps up from the bench on the steppe-
like heath: 'Enough of the blasphemous words, wretched girl, without a man, a face like fourteen days of rain, clattering- wooden-
shoes ghost, funeral bidder without a corpse, dripper of muck in
our ears, polluter of the Lord's Cross on our wall, you with the
bereft face long before the bereavement.' In the course of his litany
he begins to laugh, whereupon the rest of us, including the one so
decried, more or less join in—except her mother—whereupon he
contains himself again, or pretends to: 'Not a word of God here!
Don't any of you utter his name, no Almighty, no Merciful or Holy
Father and most of all no Supreme Being! And no talk of religion

in our midst, not one way or another. This is neither the place for praise of God nor for blaspheming God, understood? A mere "Oh God!" or "My God!" or "Dear Lord!" from you, and you—' (he begins to laugh again, infected by the rest of us, except . . . and in his turn infecting us and so on.) '—will have to reckon with me.'

Then once again the general pause. The father, once he has jumped up, has not sat down again. Now his wife, my grandmother, once she has put away her knitting things, also rises to her feet from the bench on the broad Jaunfeld. And her youngest son, likewise, stands up. It seems to me that they are all getting ready to go. Yet then I hear my blossom-young mother, who has turned to her sombre sister: 'But do you maids and labourers not also celebrate your festivals? Festivals where not only bread crusts are eaten, where not just must with ninety per cent water is drunk, where not just the linen garments rub against you, where not just lice bite into you, where not only the dung weighs heavy? Are you not perhaps the one who never finds anything to celebrate, Sister, the eternally dissatisfied farmer's drudge?'

And then the middle brother, whom to begin with I addressed as 'Valentin'. 'Ah, nothing more huggable than a farm-maid at a festival. My favourite hunting-grounds, the servant-girls. My favourite game. My fair game. None more willing. No motherly lovers. Even the ones who scored my back or whatever with fingernails grown hard from picking potatoes, from boiling pigswill, from grating sauerkraut. Even the one who spat in my mouth at a particular moment. And even the one, who, when I went behind the festival marquee with her, flicked open a flick knife at my stomach. Nothing more arousing, if I may say so. Hot, as the Americans say, hot.

In a word: divine. You're looking so enviously out of your one eye, Brother, is that so?' And the one-eyed replied curtly with 'Da'. And thereupon the very youngest of the brothers, the almost-child, to his sombre sister: 'As far as I'm concerned, Sister, go on blaspheming, unholy worrier, toximunde, sicklinde, cramphilde, demonheidi and horrortrudy. I, too, am an enemy of the time from nineteen hundred and thirty-six to nineteen hundred and thirty-six, am against numbers and against all counting. Down with Now. Down with Here.'

Yet another pause. And then, together, unhurriedly getting ready to go. My involuntary question, addressed to no one in particular: 'What did you celebrate today?' Answer, from the one-eyed, Gregor, over his shoulder: 'Our house celebration. There has never been such a thing in our district. I introduced it after my return from Yugoslavia, where it is called *slavje*, the celebration of the house and of the family. Today we are celebrating it for the first time.'

Thereupon the frowning sister: 'And, as far as I'm concerned, for the last time. To him his *slavje*—propaganda. With all his propagation of our Slavness and proclamation of our home and farmyard language as a marketplace, town and, no, not regional language but a state language, he did not bless the house with a celebration, still less a happy one, but brought discord. Him with his eternal Yugoslavia. Rash as he is, he wanted to impose his very own personal dream on all of us. It is he who sows the storm between us, the hot, heart- and head-infecting storm from the south, from the other side of the Karawanks, the jauk—even the way it's pronounced jauk!—jauk, war.'

But who intervened now, ensured with her voice alone a kind of provisional peace? Although I noticed neither gestures nor expression, I recognized after the first sentence that it was the mother of the five who was speaking—so she has no silent part in the story after all? 'Let us go home all together. It will soon be evening, and in autumn it quickly turns cool out here. The nutshells on the tree in front of the house have almost all burst by now and the first nuts have fallen off. I have put them in a basket on the dining-room table for us.' Thereupon, in the general unhurried departure, one, or other (it could even be the one whose tongue had only just been so bitter): 'And what else is there for supper, Mother?' Thereupon her mother, my grandmother: 'The freshly baked bread, warm from the oven, and with it fresh butter, churned at home, with the drops of water on top of the clot.' One, or other: 'And is that all? Stomach-ache food!' My grandmother: 'Smoked sausage and cooked ham, with the Easter horseradish—and roast pork with potatoes and roast apples. Stuffed Carinthian dumplings—' One, or other: 'With the maggots in the cheese filling?' My grandmother: '—and with it lettuce salad with caraway and cep salad in olive oil from Montenegro—' One, or other: 'Not for me!' My grandmother: 'Apple strudel in wafer dough—' One, or other: 'Like the Holy Communion wafer, without any taste.' My grandmother: '—with cinnamon and sugar and raisins from Macedonia. Halva from the last fair—' One, or other: 'Do we still have to end with something Turkish on the table? Still the Turkish threat?' My grandmother: 'Halva. Translated, it's simply "sweet", dribbled with honey—' One, or other: 'I hope not from Attica, not to mention Antalya!' My grandmother: '—extracted by your father in the bee house by the orchard.' One, or other: 'And what will there be to drink? I hope not just the elderberry juice we always get, and the must which sets one's teeth on edge?' Here, as I remember, the one-eyed or fruit farmer took over the question-and-answer game from his mother: 'Neither elderberry juice nor must—apple juice, jabol ni sok, from the jabolko, that's apple, the Welschbrunner, and, whoever wants to, can drink vino with me today, wine, one from the other side of the Karawanks—here at home—' One, or other: 'Here at home, you say, you?' The one-eyed brother: 'Yes, no vines grow here, after all—the wine from Slovenia, from Maribor, Ormož, Jeruzalem.' Thereupon, one, or several: 'Hallelujah!'

A low sun has cast its beams from the side, or from wherever, across the heath and lit up the faces of the people of my clan, while they, here and there, almost high-spiritedly, so it seems to me, set out for home. I caught just a couple of fragments of conversation: 'Red sky at night, morning's shite.' 'Red sky at dawn, night's shite.' 'Can someone knot my tie?' 'Oh, a stocking ladder!' 'I still have to feed the animals.' 'Get the first bus in the morning!' 'Will we ever all come together like this again?' (Sung) 'Should we go to the mountain meadow, should we sail across the lake . . .' They shoved one another as they went, jostled one another, walked arm in arm, tripped one another up, kicked one another, put another in a headlock, put an arm round a shoulder, carried another pickaback, twisted an arm back as if an arrest were taking place.

And so my forebears danced away, and I remained, quite alone. I followed them for a couple of steps, I think, and then paused for my part, and then cried out: 'But stay. Let us stay together. Stand by me.' And what do I, now advanced in years, see there? My blossom-young, nineteen-hundred-and-thirty-six mother, who is the only one to come back and who hurls the following at my head: 'Stop your shouting. Of course we'll stay with you, what are you thinking of? Don't you know, that we will stay with you till the end of your days, perhaps even beyond them, you great dope? That's how we're all made, and that's how it will be played here. But you, Son: Did you stay with us? Will you stay with us? Did you not always want to discard us? Get rid of us? Then stay with us. Haven't you noticed, that you are unable to do anything else, you orchard fugitive? That we, whether you like it or not, guide you? That we determine you, and not only, as you have thought at times, for the worse, you booby? Stay with us, because that's the way you're made and, accordingly, so are your fruits. And so your play, so it's up to you if you want to play. In any case, you have no choice, it's your only play, always has been, your only blueprint. Stay with us, Son.'

two

And with that she disappeared. And no one but me on the heath.
I sat down on the edge of the bench. The light changed and a breeze
came up, no storm, just strong enough to set the ninety-nine apples
in the tree in motion a little. So I sit for a long time in the steady,
hardly audible wind. So I sat or have sat there. And at some point,
after having moved my lips for a while, I will have begun to speak
out loud. 'You, Forebears—you're giving me quite a hard time.
When will you finally leave me in peace? How is that you keep on
putting in an appearance? And not only in dreams, which, unlike
most other dreams, are more real than the current date but also in
the course of the day? At the supermarket checkout or wherever
an elderly woman in a headscarf is protractedly fumbling for small
change in her purse, and grandmother mine is perhaps even more
endlessly fishing in her money sock or stocking. On the bus or
wherever a not-so-elderly man is sitting in front of me wearing a
hat that is a little too small for him, and even if he doesn't take off
the hat at all, all at once my grandfather is taking off his hat, and
I see clearly in front of me, as never in his day, his hair sticky with
sweat, the always pale forehead with the indentation made by the
sweatband, the always tanned back of the neck, the skin patterned
by the very delicate network of nothing but pentagons and hexa-
gons—hardly a four-sided figure to be seen, curious, and no rec-
tangle at all, curious. On television or wherever a young war victim

in an Arab or some other country on his way to the grave that has been dug—the youngest of our clan. In an Irish pub or wherever the reproduction of a painting of a Mass in a farmer's cottage, a table turned into an altar and at the back of the room the sideboard with the floral-pattern coffee cups, beside them the butter churn and between the priest in front at the altar and churn at the back is gathered every one of our clan, as I never saw them all together in their day, and every one of them so mutely inspired, their eyes fixed on altar table, Communion cup, priest, even on the Holy Book, fairly contradicting my mother's stories, and then again not there, when one looked more closely, curious again. In a Western or wherever—the music strikes up for a dance, and those dancing there, and how, and those who are striking up the music for the dance, and how—all of them our people, even the boobies, even the morose ones, even if there are not just seven but seventy. But back to the forebear dreams: What did I say—that they are more real than whatever else? No, more efficacious. A fine word, by the way—efficacious. Efficacious in what way? Commanding. Commanding in what way? I should. What should I? Preserve my ancestors? Too big a word and, anyway, wrong. No, there are no big words, only some in the wrong place, at the wrong moment. Venerate my precursors? I do that anyway, but that's not the point. Trace them? Let them have their say? Have them dance, as they were portrayed in the old days on the fascia boards of Slovenian bee houses? Don't know, don't know, don't know. What I know—I should. You give me a bad conscience, people, from time to time at least. Bad conscience, why? Because of my ingratitude. You're quite a bother to me, people, from time to time. On the other hand, if you don't put in an appearance for a while, neither during the day, nor in a dream, I get my bad conscience again, then, however, like this: What on earth have I done wrong, so that you don't appear to me any more? What bad thing have I done, that you don't want anything more from me, my people? What crime have I committed, that my precursors have dropped me like a lost son or like a stinking potato? My play, Mother? Without you, no play. Who plays with me? Come again. Give me something to do. Make demands of me. Draw it out of me. Don't leave me alone in my false peace.'

As desired, on cue, my mother walks onto the scene, the heath, the steppe. She still appears very young to me, only she is no longer the lively young girl from the country as in the previous scenes. She seems 'dressed to kill', as one used to say, she's wearing her hair loose, city-style, and not wound in a plait, as only a little while ago, and matching 'dressed to kill' is the foxtail round her neck, the fox head with its glass eyes at the back, the eyes sparkling when she turns full circle, tripping along, I would almost have said, in her high heels. The heels are rather high, and she makes quite a lot of noise with them, drawing a wind, in which the ninety-nine apples in the little heathland apple tree literally start rattling away as if each and every one of the pips has suddenly grown loose in its core. Or am I mistaken? And the young woman there, leaning familiarly against the little tree, is not at all my mother, of me, now advanced in years, who has now jumped up from the bench and taken a big step towards her? Anyway, I hesitate, and then I ask: 'Who are you?' And the unknown woman answers: 'You get one guess, Grandad.' And I: 'My mother.' Thereupon my mother: 'By what did you recognize me?' I: 'By your voice, my mother, without accent and without dialect.' My mother: 'Perhaps that comes from playing in the theatre group back then, before the Germans marched in. Even if we were just an amateur group, and the plays we performed were simply our old popular tales and we performed never in a theatre, at most in the parish hall, and usually in a barn somewhere, what am I saying, on a threshing floor, but every time in front of a full barn or threshing floor, and sometimes in good weather also, out in the open air, in a meadow, always in front of a full meadow, or also out here, on the open Jaunfeld, beside the apple tree, always in front of full apples. And in those days before the Germans marched in there was almost continuous good weather.' And I: 'My mother! I would have recognized you even without your voice, whatever the disguise, as a Spanish dancer with earrings as on the coffee tin we had at home, as a star in an UFA film, as a pirate's bride in a film with Errol Flynn, as a Balkan girl with the head of her lover, who fell into the ravine, in her lap, as a servant-girl in the German Reich, as avenging woman, as gardener, as murderess—even of me!—and even changed utterly, in the shape of a piebald cow with white eyelashes and without horns, changed into a well-used chopping block, into the clover leaf pattern in the wooden shithouse at home, into a ball of lightning, striking our crucifix corner.' My mother, after the two of us have settled down on the bench as we always did: 'How are you, my son?' I: 'I can't complain.' My mother: 'Yes, true, even when you were little you could never complain. And how are the women?' I: 'Bel pacific.' My mother: 'And your garden?' I: 'Bel paese. Except that the cherry tree gets too little sun, the cherries are small and sour.' My mother: 'Do you still watch so much football on TV? And when you're alone do you shout out loud enough to be heard throughout the house?' I: 'I don't watch whole games any more, not even the finals, at most one half, usually the second. And I still shout when I'm watching, except no longer in the house but somewhere in a cafe, with strangers, they're good for me, that does me good. And I still stick with the losers.' My mother: 'What are you reading at the moment? Still all those hooded crows, where the book falls out of one's hand because nothing but disaster croaks in them, of which I get more than enough in my life?' I: 'For a long time I've been reading nothing but history books.' My mother: 'So since when has my son been interested in world history?' I: 'I read about the history of our district and of our people here, as far as one can follow it back.' My mother: 'Well, that's not far . . . And what do you get from that kind of reading? Does it help you? What use can you make of any of it?' I: 'Help—none. Use—very little. It makes one helpless. Helpless, helpless. And it puts me in a rage.' My mother: 'And what do you do with your rage?' I: 'Nothing. Helpless, helpless. If I was once the earnest reader, now with local history I'm the dramatic reader. Helplessly dramatic. Because just how is it possible to dramatize the history? Or perhaps not quite so helpless—I read our history and use it as a starting point.' My mother: 'But where do you get to?' I: 'Somewhere else, perhaps out to the open sea.' My mother: 'Or into a swamp. Into a pond. Into the cesspit, where you drown. As far as I can see, you're still carrying on with your expeditions on the spot, but I hope not such dangerous ones?' I: 'Yes, dangerous. That's how it has to be, Mother.'

And again the pause, on both sides. Thereupon I: 'You talk about "back then" and "at the time", Mother. Do we lack a "once" and an "in the old days"? Why is that? Which time is it, in which we are sitting here on a bench on the Jaunfeld? Which year? What has happened so far?' (I to myself: 'Ah, back then the serial novel in the church paper, each time with the opening words: "What happened

so far!" '). My mother on our bench, her head raised, without looking at me: 'What happened so far!' My brothers are in the war,
fighting for Greater Germany, which even here . . . for sure, all
three. Even Gregor, the one-eyed, was forced to report for service,
what am I saying, was . . . allowed to be a soldier, as wireless oper-
ator or whatever. At any rate he is not yet allowed . . . to fight . . .
for his new Fatherland with a weapon in his hand. He writes nice
letters home, from Holland, where there's no front. At last, no
mountains for once, no Saualpe, no Obir and no Koschuta Mountain ridge, no Karawanks, no heaven-blocking Triglav or Dreikopf
or Triple Head. Plain after plain, all the way to the sea. The sea!
The sea! And the sky over Delft. And the tulip fields of Haaaarlem.
And the plump cows. What udders! Holland is the land flowing
with milk and honey!' She jumps up and plays her absent brother:
'And the joy of the local people at our victorious troops. The likes
of us just can't get enough of the Dutch cries of joy and other
sounds, far from the Balkans. And then the meisjes, the Dutch girls,
with their big eyes, so beautiful that they overlook my milky eye,
unlike all the girls at home! And imagine the joy on my part, dear
Parents and Sisters, when on a day pass in liberated Holland I come
upon the very tree which, at the fruit-growing school in finally-
also-liberated Yugoslavia, we were taught is   the king of apple
trees, which bears the most first-rate of all apples, the market
leader among all apples, the rustic, the rough Boskop, the boskop-
ski kosmač! Yes, the Boskop, or, more correctly, Boskoop, which
is, as its name says, a native of Holland, that is, of the village of
Boskoop, and here at last I was allowed to see such a tree in its
natural setting and to salute it, the straight-as-a-die trunk unbent
by any west wind, and its crown which promptly grows back into
a pyramid after every lightning bolt. To say nothing of the rough

fruits, which, with us at home, would surely be even rougher, blood-red marbling on the sunny side—they neither become wrinkled on the outside nor do they turn rotten from the inside. And just imagine, they keep, these Boskoopski, they remain thick and fat and marbled at least until Easter, keep perhaps until the end of the war, do konca vojne!' (She abruptly changes the register.) 'Nas ne bodo odvadili slovenščine. They won't get us to give up the Slovenian language. We shall now honour our mother tongue much more than before. No one will snatch away from us what our mother has given us. What we are, we are, and no one can dictate to us: "You are a German." Kar smo, to smo, nihčne nam ne more predpisati: "Ti si Nemec." It's a cruel time and, more than anything else, I would like to do everything wrong. "Turn an eye the other way," you say? That would be bitter for me with only one eye. I'll let you know when I'm dead. But things often happen when you least expect them, that's my hope. Damnable, how time passes—the only good thing. And so your loving son and brother, Gregor, sends greetings to you all.'

My mother will then have sat beside me again. And again we will have paused there on the open field. Finally I asked: 'You learnt the whole letter by heart, Mother?' My mother: 'I know all Gregor's forces' letters by heart, as well as the two from Benjamin as well as the one from Valentin—although there was hardly anything to remember in it. Or was there? Why did I do it? It was something I wanted to do. And then it was a pleasure. I wanted to act out for myself the news of my brothers from far away, as I had once acted out sagas and legends in my time in the amateur theatre group. And not just their news—also the language of my distant brothers, which is spoken nowhere else, our intonation, which often says something quite different from the words, and by which we recognize one another—our intonation here, that is, after all, by God or whoever, the most precious thing in our way of doing things. With it we have so far still always wanted the best for one another, even when nothing else anywhere wanted our best. I feel a need to re-enact and perform our way of speaking—whether out of love for our family or for our language I don't know. Except that our way of acting has been strictly forbidden for years, and not only since the outbreak of war. Our amateur theatre groups have been wound up, and, apart from that, also our choirs—which is no doubt fine by you, my son, for the time being you won't need to fear your mother's quavering voice any more—instead, there are quite other quaverers and quite others to fear . . .' And I: 'Once again: Which year since the birth of Christ am I supposed to imagine now? And what else has happened to our family in the meantime?' And my mother: 'Let's say it's the year nineteen forty-two, and again late summer, as six years ago, or early autumn, the corn, apart from the ajda—oh, forbidden word! our language forbidden—the buckwheat, gathered in, the cattle still in the meadow. World war for three years now, but hardly making itself felt in the district, at most in the absence of the young men of the locality—to make up more and more young dancers from elsewhere . . . Our Benjamin a common soldier in the East somewhere. But he has not been allowed on the front line yet, not yet. In the only photograph, he's sitting in uniform and the rest on an old-fashioned heavy Swift bike, ready for action, so to speak, in fact he's crouching on it looking a right fool—if you know what I mean.' (And now my mother has stood up again and is copying or playing the part of the absent second brother.) 'So far the war has only been good to Benjamin. He has, so he writes home, grown up thanks to the war. And, light-shy as he used to be, he has learnt to appreciate the sun up there in the tundra. After three months of darkness, he writes, it's returned today. The first spot of sun since seventeenth November. Hooray, here comes the sun! Above all, he doesn't feel disgust at anything any more. Rice pudding—one of my favourite foods. A comrade's attached ear lobes—good enough to kiss. Webbing between the fingers of another comrade—the sky shines through it. The sergeant major's bark—the call to open-air Mass. The heaps of excrement in the latrine pit—remind him of the funny curly tails of the piglets in the pigsty at home. Day and night marches of fifty kilometres— nema problema, converted into versts, it's far fewer. In general— being able to say "verst" instead of "kilometre"! "Dnieper, Don, Volga and Amur" instead of "Gurk, Glan, Gail and Lavant"! "Voskressenje" instead of "Resurrection"! I enjoy singing now, too. I even lead the singing in our platoon, discovered my voice while requisitioning food in Russian villages, the war has made a tenor of me! And just once you should see your little brother, the one with two left feet, dancing. Out here in the field I dance like crazy with the girls. And no girl that doesn't like the language of our home better than the usual one in the army and me along with it—believe me or not. Sonja! Natasha! Asja! There you see it—the war a poet has made of me. Our Jaunfeld, our district, at last has the one person it's been missing since the last Ice Age even if his absence has largely gone unnoticed—the poet, I! If I could I would write all my forces' letters to you on white birch bark, on which the lines themselves are already a poem.' (My mother abruptly changes her register again, reads between the lines as it were.) 'We're not short of birch trees in Russia. And we've all become slim as birches. Slim is the new fashion. Marching, marching until everything goes white before one's eyes. White by day, white in the night and again white by day. Marching, marching, past the empty lines of birch bark, past the empty lines of the potato fields, past the empty lines of the cabbage and turnip fields, past the empty lines of the thousand empty villages, until with all the empty lines we see nothing but empty lines, and on and between and behind all the empty lines no "on" and "between" and "behind" any more and no world. Will the old, the good days ever come again? Yes, the old, the good! And so, greetings to you all from your tundra lad Benjamin.' And at that then my mother, as if not acting: 'Yes, without the war, we would never have written to each other. Without the war, I would have nothing written by my brothers. Ah war! Praise be to you, war! Thanks to you, my brothers saw something of the world.'

Here both mother and son paused again. The young woman beside me abruptly emerged from it and tripped over to the edge of the steppe-like field. And just as abruptly she turned to someone invisible, at least to me: 'Sig hail, Herr Obersturmkommandant! We are joyful to have you between us. Well-waxed boots are yours. Prosim, but do, so that I am fearful of you, Herr Understorm warden! May I storm to your brown side! And may your ticket-home wound not be shot in the foot! Hitro, hurry and hold out hand to us, before maybe Volkssturm storm onto heath against last róža!' The answer is not long in coming—a voice from the direction in which my mother was speaking, or from somewhere else, which talks back in best High German: 'There you have your Volkssturm, Frau Untermensch: Learn German before you do anything else. Your disguise: perfect—well done. Dressed like Eva Braun and with the hairstyle of Heidemarie Hatheyer. Even your voice—not exactly Zarah Leander and not Lale Andersen either, but still—now I can't remember the name. Your language, it gave you away. Language? Don't make me laugh. And don't try to talk yourself out of it by saying you didn't know the decree that here only German is to be spoken in public. What, you dare to object, by saying that this is not a public place? You have the cheek to wallow in your Untermensch gibberish in front of German speakers? Over the Wurzen Pass with you. Heave ho, over the Hunsrück Hills with you underhand Hunnish hounds! Away with you down to Triglav, to Trigon, to Lake Trasimenus, to the Tuaregs—so that we native speakers can be by ourselves at last—'

And only then did I realize it was my mother herself who had been speaking there, as a kind of ventriloquist. The young woman has tripped back towards me, her old son, but then has remained at a distance on the broad, slightly sloping heath scene. I spoke to her over my shoulder: 'Why have you stopped imitating the enemy, Mother? For a long time now I've been lacking an antagonist in our story. One who stirs things up, causes confusion. Or asks the awkward questions. Who doesn't just open his mouth, but his jaws wide. And seeks whom he may swallow up.' My mother, in her turn, speaks over her shoulder to me—the eyes of the fox and her own: 'My son, don't worry. Patience—but that was never your strength. The antagonist, or the antagonists, they have been taken into account from the beginning.' And I: 'How do you know that?' And my mother: 'I don't know, I have a feeling, something tells me. And something tells me that they will come from our own ranks, from our own stock, possibly from our own house. In the course of events it will all become clear to you. It may be, that on some not-so-distant day I myself will also be found on the opposite side or will have lost myself to it, believing, in my eternal high spirits and my eternal good cheer, which always take hold of me, that we all belong together and that we're all good for one another, and that, basically, war or no war, everything on earth is good . . . Strange. In all my life I've never been sad. Hungry, yes. Half frozen, yes. Lost in the woods, yes. Bitten by a dog, look, here, yes. Kicked in the ribs, here and here, by a horse, yes. Stung between the eyes by a hornet and been blind for a whole month, not just in one eye, yes. But sad—never ever. It's unnatural really, isn't it? My eternally sad sister, on the other hand, my grim-browed sister, worse than just sad, even if she has no reason for it—except she almost always has a reason . . . "You and your cheerfulness!" she snaps at me as if Miss Cheerful can only be her enemy? A mere figment of an enemy? Yes. But it can happen that a real enemy comes of such a figment. Possible that right here and now I'm on the brink of becoming an enemy and not just to my sombre sister. It's enough when I see myself in the mirror, my clothes, my new hairstyle, the mascara, the lipstick . . . The enemy of the clan, of the tribe, of the people from here—I? How strange, that even this awful thought does not make me sad. I, the enemy of us all—awful. And yet at no moment does it impede my joy in life. So it's my joy in life which in time of war makes of me an enemy? Don't know, God knows. How surprised I am, that I'm not sad. Will it all become clear to me in the course of events?'

And once again there's a pause. Then my mother turns towards the spot at which she imitated the voice before: 'The one whose voice I ventriloquized over there, he was no enemy. It was certainly someone very bad. But I don't see him as our antagonist. He's no good for that. He's not worthy of our history. Yes, you heard right—not worthy! If I could I would just laugh at him and at all his superiors along with him, right up to the topmost superior high up in his hunting-dog kennels in the Dwarf Mountains. And the whole district here will attest that I am a past master at having a good laugh at someone. I've even tried it out on one or another. But there it didn't work. And what does that mean? It certainly made the person concerned go off with his tail between his legs, for a while, but it hardly made matters easier for me. So I was weighed down, I? Strange, once again. The things one can discover by talking! I had accordingly wanted to free myself by having a good laugh, I? Liberating? Not a bit. And so that's how the ventriloquism came about. Unplanned—every time the control clowns start hitting out all over the place with their clubs it comes out of my stomach—which, actually, should serve for something else— . . . ventriloquizing, mimicking, how liberating it is, when one's all alone! So am I lonely? Strange. The things one can discover by talking. Mimicking as relief, momentarily. Admittedly, you all know very well, mimicking like that only works when it happens in passing. As soon as I continue deliberately, or even set out to do it from the start, it's no good. It doesn't cut deep. Imitation like that only depresses me all the more. So depression also comes into it, in the breezy early autumn of nineteen hundred and forty-two? Strange. The things . . . —In the course of events will it all . . . ?' This last my mother did no more than mutter to herself. And finally then, if I heard it right: 'Back then in our amateur theatricals, there was no question of imitating someone . . . It wasn't necessary yet either, as now in the war, with all the alien, bad, hobnailed boots, raised whips and rifle-butt voices . . .'

Pause again? Now there's no time for it. Because my mother's sister, called 'Ursula' at the beginning comes running, in the dress almost of a pig-maid, wearing the classic wooden shoes and so on, and instantly attacks the other woman, the one dressed as if for the big city. Tearing at hair, dealing blows with a stick—even if only in the air—elbowing, punching, tripping up, throwing to the ground— all of it silent. Only then does the farm-maid begin to speak, her words directed at the woman who has immediately stood up again: 'That's for you smiling at one of them from outside. That's for you going with one of the others. While I spend the nights in the straw behind the goatshed, you romp about on the double bed of the Tigerwirt Hotel with your German billy goat from the Reich. While our parents slave away alone at home, on the brink of exhaustion, close to despair because of their three sons recruited by force into the Third Reich, the two of you sit side by side on City Beach Berlin and watch your cigarette smoke trails, as they sail away from the tips of your two cigarettes, side by side, out across the Reich's lakes Wörthersee, Ossiachersee, Turnersee and Keutschachersee. While our brothers out there in Holland, up there in Norway, over there in Russia are not just forbidden to speak our language, vital in such a different way, a help in need, but also to sing it, forbidden on pain of detention the baritone of the one, the tenor of the second, the bass of the third, you two fine folk warble the "Habanera" inside at the table of the officers' mess, and you hum the "White Elderflower" into his ear lobe and he for his part dribbles his "White Lilac Time" through your rags right onto the skin. How could you just forget who you are? Who we are here? What we represent? What our place is on earth? You betrayed us? Worse— you forgot us, beautiful Sister! Looking for love as ever in another language, in another land? Why? Yes, why?'

While the farm maid daughter talks in this way, her parents, my grandparents, have appeared on the scene out of the background, in country working clothes this time, apron, rubber boots and so on. They have become distinctly older and now appear about the same age as me, their grandson. My grandfather is holding a letter in each hand, evidently forces' post, evidently unopened. The two have listened in silence. What they are hearing appears to be new to them. Accordingly, the father speaks as follows: 'Is it true, what your sister is saying? Is it true that you're going out with one of the others?' And thereupon the woman with the fox: 'Yes, I'm going out with one of the others. And he's going out with me.' Her father: 'What does that mean?' His daughter: 'I love him. And I think he loves me, too.' Her father: 'You think. Love! I don't want to hear the word. No one here has ever talked about love before. And as long as I have any say in the matter, no one here will use such a word either, not love and not ljubezen.' She: 'Then, dear Mother, dear Father, I'll just say it another way—' And she unbuttons her loose overcoat—a big bulging stomach. Whereupon her father and her farm-maid sister take a step backwards, while her mother, my grandmother, steps forward, silently, and I? I have stood up from the bench in the middle of the steppe-like heath, equally silent. Whereupon my mother beckons me to come closer: 'Did you not always want to see yourself filmed in rewind, my son, as adolescent, as child, as infant and back even before your birth? Here you have the film. Look, there in my stomach—you!' Whereupon I look. Whereupon the pregnant woman invites me: 'Place your hand here!' Whereupon I recoil. Whereupon my grandfather says: 'Well, if that's the way it is . . .' Whereupon the sombre sister asks: 'When did it happen?' Whereupon my mother replies: 'Happen? In late spring. Vigredi. Between lilac- and elderflower-blossom time. Between midnight and four o'clock in the morning. In the Tigerwirt, or where we happened to be walking and standing. Love—my fate. And our Jaunfeld has only seen something more beautiful than my stomach at all holy times!'

Thereupon once again a pause. And then my grandfather sits down beside me on the bench and also beckons his daughter, pregnant with me, to sit down. He opens one of the letters and gives it to her to read. First she says the name of the sender: 'Valentin.' And only when she has read the letter silently to herself—it's not at all long—does she read it to the remainder of the clan, this time without acting out or being her brother's voice, first of all saying: 'Strange. The great ladies' man is the only one of our brothers who doesn't write anything about a war girlfriend.' —'My dear family! I am doing splendidly. But I know anyway that you are not worrying about me—if you were, then you would be the only ones. I, at least, have never had any worries about myself, don't even know what that is, a worry, in our farmyard language a word that sounds harsh to the ear: skrb, otrok ga skrbi, he's worried about the child—' The reader interrupts: 'The censor crossed that out, but if one knows, then it's still legible.' And she continues reading: 'Nothing can happen to me, I already knew that when I was little, when the lightning struck the threshing floor, and then later, when the Heimwehr Militia man or whatever he was, perhaps he was just a jealous husband, shot at me. Where we are—' Again, she interrupts: 'The letter was written in early summer, took two months to arrive,' and continues reading: 'Where we are, the sun still shines at midnight. My problem is the mosquitos, they seem to like my blood more than that of my comrades. The polar bears aren't expected until winter, but you know that I'm a born hunter. The British are still keeping their heads down, the only thing we hear from them are the names of their football teams, and they are a help when I can't get to sleep at night: Aston Villa—Wolverhampton Wanderers—Tottenham Hotspurs—West Bromwich Albion—Leeds United —Manchester United—Red Stars Newcastle—Partizan Belfast . . .' The reader: 'Here, too, the censor has blacked out words, and I hope I haven't made mistakes deciphering the names.' She reads to the end (as if between the lines?): 'How boring war is—above all, boring. Every day the same. No Sunday, no holiday. How many useful things could be done at home, which would be of benefit to the country in quite a different way. Coming home, working! How I long for a proper day's work instead of being bored until final victory! I miss you, Sister. I was always able to tell you everything. But the time will come again. And I'll come back as a millionaire. Hail to you all, hail to you, Valentin, Son of the Northern Light—'

Pause. Then my grandfather opens the second letter and hands it to my mother to read. Once again she begins by reading inwardly and right away interrupts herself: 'Strange, it's not Benjamin himself writing—' And then one can only hear something like a gasp, a sound, like one of those sounds, whether of horror or repugnance or also of pleasure and of delight, which were altogether one of the common family characteristics. And so now a whole chorus, Grandfather, Grandmother, Sister and even I, unborn, gasp in response to my mother. And then the pregnant woman stands up and removes her shoes and her coat and throws them this way and that way, far away, out of sight. And after that she puts up her hair, almost ceremoniously, as it was at the beginning. And the letter? I don't remember—but perhaps, with the gasp, I went blind for a moment? What I then see—the farm-maid sister holding the letter. And what I hear from her: 'I knew it.' Did she then read out the letter? It seems to me, only in fragments: '. . . to his last breath, showing courage in the face of the enemy . . . enemy . . . did not suffer . . . for Fürer and Fatalant . . . will always honour his sacrifice . . . may the enemy soil lie light . . . light . . . light . . . light . . .' And after that? Again a shared clan or even people's chorus note—and I part of it once more—now admittedly no longer a gasp, rather something else monosyllabic, between monosyllabic whimpering and howling, unpleasant to hear for ears attuned to mourning, on the verge of embarrassing, but that's how it was with us and how it is, and apart from which our people's chorus immediately fell silent once again after this one note.

Who is the first to be heard after the fraction of a minute or of a whole year? My grandfather, and if, as events unfolded, he so far cursed more to himself, now for the first time he curses out loud: 'May they all be cursed. May Satan take them all, from Arnulf to Ziegfried, from the Annelieses to the Zieglindes. May Germany, Germany become nothing and less than nothing in the world. From the Maas to the Memel nothing and nothing and once again nothing, and in between, here, there, a dried mouse dropping, a tapeworm in a chamber pot, a rusty doorbell in a broken toothbrush glass in dirty snow. Never again see someone Djerman with his Djerman skull, his Djerman legs, with his Djerman bone structure, with his Djerman parting in his hair, with his Djerman bicycle clip round his Djerman trouser leg, with his Djerman shoe size for his Djerman feet. Never again hear someone Djerman, with his airsplitting speech, with his one-note tuning-fork voice, with his eardrum-bursting bawling, with his sonorous chalky gluttonous fluting. May they be torn apart in the air, the Germans. Buried by bombs from Mars. In the firestorm at last no more than a shadow, their first, their last.' And then he takes a big step towards his pregnant daughter: 'And cursed be the little love worm in your love stomach. Cursed be the fruit of your womb. The Lord has given, the Lord has taken, cursed be the name of the Lord in all eternity!' And he raised his arm as if to strike, and I on the bench—did I cower? did I recoil? And my mother? Did not budge from the spot, did not bat an eyelash.

It was my grandmother who then called her husband to order, by placing her arm on his shoulder and saying: 'So Benjamin's baptismal candle has become his funeral candle. Let us go home and light it. Besides, the animals have to be fed, and the eggs in the hay need to be collected before the polecat sucks them dry. Oh, how clumsy he was. As altar boy he knocked over the thurible during Mass and was picking up the individual grains of incense until the final blessing, and he missed the priest's fingers when he poured out the wine, and he didn't stop ringing the bell for the transformation of the bread into Christ's body right through the Lord's Prayer up to the Agnus Dei. And yet how much strength he had in his hands. Do you remember how you once gave him the huge key to unlock the must cellar? He didn't get the door open, it's true, but broke the key in half, that's how strong he was. We remember his clumsiness? Yes, now especially, don't we?' My grandmother and her husband slowly get going, away from the steppe-like heath, towards home? As they do so she continues: 'The bread is still in the oven, it mustn't turn black. And once he was a dwarf in a school play and for the whole play he just sat there cross-legged and did nothing but sew, and was constantly pricking himself and afterwards he said: "That's because Mother was watching!" His best jacket in the wardrobe on the gallery above the chicken coop—he' (she points at me) 'should get that, when the time comes, after the war one day, and also the confirmation watch, isn't that right? But look, over there, a hare running zigzag. And how beautiful the clouds are, with a golden border as on the altar painting in the parish church. And the grass is already wet from the evening dew. Yes, a page has been torn from the book of our life, rip. I can't believe that he's dead. God loves to return, the priest said in the last sermon. Is it true? And tomorrow is Sunday. Don't forget the card game in the afternoon. Tarock! There's a smell of autumn. Do you smell it, too?' Thereupon her husband: 'You with your eternal conciliation. With your delusion of peace. Peace on earth? Impossible.'

Meanwhile the two sisters have in the same way started on the way home. And again the general departure has something of a dance about it, a dance—if such a thing exists—of mourning. At the edge of the field, the sombre sister picks up the long pale overcoat thrown away by my mother and pulls it on over her farm-maid's clothes, and says: 'This will be my magic coat. It will make me invisible, in winter, in the forests, in our forests!, in the mountains, our mountains!, in the snow.' Thereupon my mother: 'So that means—' Her sister: 'Yes, that's what it means. I'm marching to war. I'm going to war. I'm somersaulting to war, to mine, to ours. One of our Green Cadres in the forests of the Petzen Peak, by Kömmel, of Mount Ursula.' Then my mother: 'There's no more happiness for me. I shall never be happy again.' And thereupon her sister: 'Are you sure? You—without happiness?' And thereupon—I can no longer see either—still my mother: 'Yes . . . no . . . yes!'

three

And again I am left behind as the only one on the bench in the middle of the Jaunfeld. Wind, noticeably stronger than the first time I remained here alone. From the ninety-nine apples something like a tinkling. At some point I began to tell a story. At first, however, I talk more to myself. And only then do I begin to express myself, loud and clear—as far as someone like me is capable of doing. As I continue it's almost as if I'm making a statement, for moments at a time like a newsreader, or, rather, I'm playing the part, as I increasingly make slips of the tongue, jabber, stutter, get stuck again and again. And so I play and say and stutter: 'Green Cadres—green is clear enough, the forest, the forests. But cadre? Are they not senior officers? Commanders? As far as I know, those who embellished themselves with the name Green Cadres were nothing but a helpless and lost little troop of fellows—at the beginning hardly a woman among them—who had fled into the forests because they didn't want to be in the war. The world war of the Swabians, the švabi, as the Germans were called at home, was not theirs. And, apart from that, no war had ever been theirs, ours. Nevertheless "troops", here and there a couple who had come together deep in the evergreen and were waiting to see how things would continue. Before that, each one had gone into the forests quite on his own, blindly. Anything but the war. First of all, hide away alone in the undergrowth, not exactly in panic, but, in the early days there, at any rate, without any hope whatsoever. They had not always been so lacking in hope since nineteen thirty-three. At the beginning of the war they had still looked to the Russian big brother, also language brother, for support. But then he unexpectedly made a pact with the Swabians. No other way out for the abandoned except off into the forests—into the deadest of dead ends? Yes, for a while. And I would like to know how these isolated few then found the strength to whistle themselves together through the spruce, pine and fir needles. What's certain is that almost all of the fellows had healthy bronchial tubes. According to our historians—bearing in mind that the later history writers were as a rule the Green Cadres themselves—in peacetime, the men of the forest, when their language was still tolerated, had one and all sung in the church choir and, curiously enough, the solo singer in the choir later, in the cadre troop, became something like a commander. And what's also certain is that at first, perhaps, hopelessness dominated, but not helplessness. Because the fugitives in the homeland forests knew every possible hiding place and knew how to provide for themselves. Quite a few of them had worked as woodcutters before the war. And most of them had hunted on the side, not as hunters appointed by the count or some other landowner, whatever are you thinking of—no, as poachers. Every one of them was able to use a hunting rifle, and those of them who had then been forced into the war and after home leave, or whatever it was called, went into the mountain forests, likewise familiar with hand grenades, machine guns and sub-machine guns. They remained a lost troop, nevertheless, lost in what had been their own land, which for them continued to be their own, more than ever! To have given themselves a name, that was at any rate more than nothing. But these Green Cadres—what could they do? How could they fight? How offer resistance, this group, which, despite the proud name, was isolated, few in number, to a might which would hold them fast at even a first step away from the forest's edge. How resist, or simply just survive? Things only changed when the omnipresent resistance across the border in occupied Yugoslavia, which the Green Cadres wandering in the forest only knew about by hearsay, spread northwards to them across the Karawanks, and they saw themselves, unexpectedly, as part of the Europe-wide Resistance. Away with the loudmouth name! They were no longer Green Cadres, who, beyond the name, didn't know what to say and what to do, but part of the Résistance against the world-conquering monsters and no-good-doers, a host, an army, from the Peloponnese north to the Svinjska planina, from the Kor Alps west to La Rochelle—the Army of the Partisans and "Partisans" is what they were called now, together with the rest and also taking pride, in a different way from before, in letting the superior force call them "bandits". Never had they and their forefathers conducted war in this land? Now it had come, their war, yes, their war, led by the local former church choir singers, by the tenors, baritones, basses, who as partisans carried on the only organized, militarily continuous resistance within the borders of the Thousand Year Reich, as the army of partisans and, finally, also as victors. The only question is: What did the war do for them and what the victory, for them and you and me? The only question is: What kind of peace was it after war and victory, and was it one at all? The question is: Where are the fighters, where have they gone? The question is, we ask, you ask, they ask, ask whom or what, ask Heaven, ask the SINGER sewing machine, ask the rusty sledge, ask everyone, just don't ask me!—Now, finally, I wanted to speak in the plain language which I'm always accused of avoiding—again, no good . . .'

When I look over my shoulder I see my mother's two surviving brothers standing close behind me. No doubt they already came onto the scene a while ago. But once again I was so wrapped up in myself that I didn't notice their approach. Both are evidently on home leave. For Gregor, the one-eyed, the eldest, it's not the first day at home, he's wearing civilian clothes, country Sunday clothes and, what do I see here?, is pushing something like a pram back and forward while holding pruning shears, or whatever they are, in his other hand. Valentin, by contrast, seems to have just got off the postbus after a long journey by ship and by train—he is still in the uniform of the mountain troops and is weighed down by something like a sailor's kitbag. Only now do I also hear, from here and there on the broad Jaunfeld, the distant holiday sound of church bells. One of the main religious festivals is perhaps under way. Whitsun? Assumption Day? (The way the fields are turning green fits more with Whitsun.) For the two brothers I don't exist, not at any rate as the long-adult person of the present. They talk as if without witnesses, and yet it seems to me as if I should bear witness to them. And from time to time I did pull out my notebook and wrote down what was being said. Like the following: Gregor to Valentin: 'No toes frozen off, Valentin?' Valentin to Gregor: 'I regularly rub them with snow. That keeps the circulation going.' Gregor: 'My ears are still buzzing from my radio equipment. Yet I've already been home on leave for a week.' Valentin: 'At home on leave at the same time as you, Gregor. Who would have expected it? The army commanders mean us well.' Gregor: 'They could have meant even better if they had exempted Benjamin, not yet twenty years of age and with a crippled index finger, from active service.' Valentin, after a period of silence, in a different voice which represents that of his fallen brother: 'Shooting is for the others. When *I* squeeze, then at most when I'm shitting or with Tatjana.' Gregor, likewise in the other voice: 'But she doesn't let me, more's the pity.' Both together playing the dead brother: 'If I had a Mauser, I would shoot not left nor right, I would not shoot in the morning, I would not shoot at night, I sure would make a bang, but not the one you think.' Valentin: 'And do you remember how he started as an apprentice to the smith right after his last school day?' Gregor: 'He had no sooner taken his satchel off his back than his blue apprentice overalls, with the legs too short and the sleeves too short, were slipped onto him.' Valentin: 'It was a very cold morning, and not just for summer, when he set out for the smithy.' Gregor: 'And do you remember what he said?' And again the pair play their dead brother: 'Gentlemen, that's enough shivering for me, for now and for all eternity!' Then Valentin: 'And do you still remember, what our dear sister wrote to us about him, when after a year of taiga and tundra war he for the first—' Gregor: '—and last time—' Valentin: 'was home on leave? How our sister thought that after such an experience his squeamishness or his fussiness must have been puffed away, been burnt out of him.' Gregor: 'And how to welcome him home she placed a cup of coffee in front of him with a single, a minute shred of milk skin on it—' Valentin: '—and how he immediately pushed the cup away and said—' Again the two of them in unison playing their dead brother: ' "—Born yesterday was I!" ' And again the two brothers fell silent, and nothing happened except that the pram was still being pushed back and forward. And then Gregor: 'It's funny, that in our clan it's always the same couple of stories that keep on being told. And all of them are short, and with none of them does one really know why they're going round, what's so worth passing on about them, what they have to do with each other anyway, apart from, perhaps, the never-ending revulsion.' Valentin: 'The story about our father when he was a child, how he was sent to the priest with the annual contribution in kind, a bulky sack of apples in the wheelbarrow—' Gregor: '—in the carriola—' Both together: '—and how our father then says to the priest: "Father, here I bring you the apples from our shithouse tree!"' Gregor: 'And the story about the imbecile farm-maid, whom someone had made pregnant, and the child was taken away from her after the birth. It was raised by the farm family, and one of the farm daughters took the place of the mother. And, one day, the child was already able to speak, it got stuck in the meadow fence when it was playing and couldn't get free, and the bull was already pawing the ground in front of the child and the imbecile heard the child's cries far far away and she ran over and pulled the child out of the fence, and later, at home, the child asked his supposed mother, the farmer's daughter, that is.' And again the two brothers speak in unison: '"Mother, why does the imbecile have such soft hands?"' This was once again followed by a silence, and then one of the two, I no longer remember which, asked the other: 'Do you think we'll ever sing in the choir again?' The other: 'No. At any rate not in any church choir.' They now attempt, with the last sentence of the story just told, a kind of choral singing as a duet: it doesn't work, once again and once again—notes discordant enough to put one's hands over one's ears. Thereupon one brother: 'It seems I can only sing alone now—if at all.' And the other: 'I'm the same.' Then once again nothing happens except the pram being pushed back and forward, seconded by the clacking of the pruning shears. Valentin: 'Why have you got the pruning shears with you? Is it already time to prune the trees?' Gregor: 'No. And yet, since I've been on leave, I constantly want to cut something back. Thin out. Create views. Or cut off the willy of the rascal here. Hear him bawl, me, his unwilling godfather. Untimely! I always hated the in-between times of the year—the cherries harvested long ago or eaten by the blackbirds, the cherry trees throughout the land empty, nothing but trembling leaves and the empty stalks with their dried-up stones, and no other fruit ripe apart from the pale early apples which don't even have a name—a Communion wafer is a delicacy by comparison. And now, on top of that, this nappy shitter here. Into the ailing cherry-tree shade with you, ailing infant.' Valentin: 'And you say that, you who were always the gentlest of us all? Good nature in person? Warm-hearted? The one who reconciled us every time? Who was always just and fair?' Gregor: 'I don't want to be the one who's always fair any more. Not at this time at least. And I have resolved to be irreconcilable towards the enemy, have resolved to be merciless, am resolved to be an enemy myself.' Valentin: 'You and resolving—nothing more alien. You and enemy—nothing more absurd. You and the mere word "enemy"—the foreign language of foreign languages coming from your mouth, in your—Reich, yes, dear Brother, in our Reich.' Thereupon Gregor: 'I spit on my Reich—' And it seems to me that he really did spit, in every point of the compass. 'I'm a desperado by now and nothing more. It goes against the grain, that I see the enemy even in this cheesy little infant. But that's how it is, that's how it has come to be. There he lies, beams at me, grabs at me with his little grabbing hands, not made for any honest work, burbles at me with his pale lips, from which it is clear that in all eternity not a word in our holy mother tongue will emerge, never mind a sound, not even a murmur—doesn't stop waving at me with his little trembling ears, transparent and fatty as grease-proof paper—the enemy is listening. Yes, to me he represents the enemy, the cuckoo, who will throw all of us, whose homes are here, out of the nest down to the last chirrup and piece of fluff. Mite, early form of the greater enemy, of the usurper. Enemy of our family—enemy of our people. Out of the cradle—into the dog kennel with the bastard.' As he spoke, he pushed the pram with 'me' in it back and forward, even if not exactly gently, finally even with a kick, and after another short silence Valentin will have objected: 'Is it not a pity, Gregor, that you're spoiling the last day of your leave for yourself and me and all of us?' Thereupon his elder brother: 'Yes, the front lines are already waiting, in every direction of our sky, which is our homestead here, naša hiša, naša domovina—the Eastern Front, the Western Front, your Northern Front in Norway, my Southern Front in the Balkans. But they can all wait!' Thereupon Valentin: 'What are you trying to say?' Gregor: 'That I'm going to change fronts, sides, today.' Valentin: 'You, you're going to go into the forests?' Gregor: 'Yes, I or someone, or something.' Valentin: 'You, you're ready, to kill?' Gregor: 'Yes, I, or someone.' Valentin: 'You're going to shoot at people? You, who disappeared into the attic every time the pig was slaughtered? Who ran away when Father cut the throat of a hare? Who even today hides behind our mother when the decapitated hen rushes back and forth across the yard? Who breathes on every frozen bee to bring it back to life? Who every time wants to get the mouse away from the cat? Who would like to stick back together with his spit every worm cut in two by the shovel? You, draw the pin of a hand grenade and throw it through the open window at the card-playing country police?' Gregor: 'Yes, I. I will do it!' Valentin: 'How are you going to aim at all, half-blind as you are? Even before you lost your eye, you always missed at the fairground shooting gallery and never got an artificial rose or a teddy bear. I was the one who always hit the mark. And when our father and I wanted to take you poaching, you had something that urgently needed doing in the orchard every time, a branch that was evidently too heavy and that needed supporting, a must pear that needed grafting.' Gregor: 'That was once upon a time. Didn't we constantly say and reproach one another, because in our family, in our clan, in our people, there's a lack of resolve? That for that reason, too, we're children without luck? That all together we've never achieved anything much, because we've never, never ever decided for or against anything?' Valentin: 'What kind of decision, Brother? Against foreign rule? Against the masters from the Isar, from the Main, from the Rhine and from the Elbe imposed on us?' Gregor: 'For example.' Valentin: 'Not a chance. Nema šanse. The power of the authorities allows no leeway, least of all the current German ones. Un-German activities? Driven out in the twinkling of an eye, and our people here, as many as you like, as mere labourers and odd-job men and all with our beautiful local names. What kind of decision, Brother? For our mother, father, child and house, hearth and farmyard language, for our original Slav or Illyrian or Ostrogothic or whatever accents, through which apparently, so you maintain, the soul of folks like us is expressed, which apparently is the language of love and of the land itself? For the language which gives me, for example, at most a little cowshed warmth for

a while?' Gregor: 'Yes, for the language, my, our language.'
Valentin: 'Our language, too, dear Brother, dragi brat—it hasn't a
chance. As for me—I made my decision long ago. And my decision
is—the West. Westworld. Away from the confinement of the mountains and of the stubborn language of the mountains. Into the open.
Become a citizen of the world. For me, personally, the war has so
far almost only meant good things, isn't that so? To me, even Germany is already the West, open to the world. Don't we say here: "Out
to Germany!"? Out in Germany, don't we? And going towards the
Balkans, on the other hand, we say: "Down to Maribor, down to
Ljubljana." To say nothing of Belgrade—down, down. And when
we talk about our own places—right in Eisenkappel, right in Zell
Winkel, right in Gallizien, right in Heiligenblut, right in the Lavant
Valley, right in Möll Valley, right in Bären Valley. Don't we? Germany, at any rate seen from here, outside. The West. And England!
To say nothing of America! What, above all, have I learnt thanks
to the war, apart from chess—English! That's the language for me,
dear Brother. You want to know how I managed it? Military secret.
Love me tender. Oh my darling Clementine. Long-distance infor-
mation, give me Memphis Tennessee. In the midnight hour, I gonna
shake my tambourine. Come closer. Do you feel it? Knocking on
Heaven's door . . . Long as I can see the light . . . Shall we gather at
the river—' He interrupts himself: 'Do you realize, dear Brother,
that resistance, if it wants to be successful, necessarily turns into
war? Do you want war?' And thereupon Gregor: 'This one, yes.
I've always been ready to love my enemies. But the present ones—
no!—No people in the whole world was more peace*ful*, more peace-
able than we were here. We, yes, we embodied, lived, played, acted,
danced, performed peace on earth! And now—we must, yes, must
embody war here, we must!'

To be added is that, during the scene, my mother must have made an appearance from somewhere, unnoticed both by me on the bench as well as by her two brothers, one taking his leave of home and the other just arrived. Now she calls out the name of the latter, and we others look over our shoulders at her. She's wearing the maid's clothes of her sister, which on her don't look workaday at all. At the same time as she called, she took off her bee veil, or whatever it is—otherwise she would hardly have been recognizable. Valentin slips off his military bag, and she strides towards him, puts her arm round him and rests her forehead against his. The clan's wind wailing, see above, in chorus—so *this* choir still manages it—in which Gregor, too, joins in, but right away breaking off again. His sister hands Valentin something that he bites into or perhaps licks—a honeycomb? Yes, because she then says: 'A good year for honey. Especially the honey from the flowering ash, each white blossom full of juice, every rib full of honey.' Gregor: 'Down there in the Balkans, one is not welcomed with honey but with bread and salt.'

And then a silence again, until Valentin points at or into the pram: 'And the man to go with the child?' His sister: 'Home to the Reich.' Valentin: 'Fled or forced to go?' She: 'Think what you like.' Valentin: 'As for me—so far I've always taken flight, even before the question arose.' She: 'Quiet! It was love. It is love.' Valentin: 'If our father hears that: "Love" . . . How long were you together?' She: 'A night.' Valentin: 'A single night?' She: 'Yes. And it counts more than ten thousand others.' Gregor, butting in: 'Curious mathematics. How does it count? Where is it written? Where is it entered?' She: 'In the Book of Life.' Gregor: 'Are you sure?' She:

'Yes! There it stands, for ever.' (Finally, Valentin joined in and then, bent over the pram, goes on talking solo.) 'The result does give one some idea—how blissfully our bastard is lying there. The face admittedly of a small rat. But how that face is creased with laughter, at nothing, nothing at all! Cheerful and delightful. Probably he already spent all the nine moons in the womb—' She: '—under my heart!' Valentin: '—under your heart, looking forward to coming out into the sun, could hardly wait, and from the third or fourth month was already hopping impatiently up and down in your stomach?' She: 'That's right.' Valentin: 'Are you sure he's not an imbecile?' She: 'Yes. No.' Valentin: 'I see a bad moon rising. A bee will sting him on his lower lip and he'll be an elephant man for a whole year. He'll have ingrown toenails and walk barefoot until his last year at primary school. At seven, always looking at the sky, he'll fall into a manure pit and almost drown in it, and at ten, for the same reason, a pigeon will shit his eyes shut and he'll be blind from the Nativity of Mary until All Souls'. After that, however, he'll only look at the ground in front of him and everything will take a turn for the better—he'll find money just like that, first coins, then banknotes, finally gold. He'll be the very first of our leaden clan to have silver and gold under his feet. He'll be our first numbers man. I'm telling you—one day he'll be something very special—a bookkeeper! Maybe a bank clerk!' And abruptly he turns to my mother: 'And how will we two go on, my dear?' Thereupon my mother: 'Not at all, dear. Just the same as from the start.' Thereupon Valentin: 'Ah, longing. You, love the German? Unfathomable.' Thereupon my mother: 'Yes, unfathomable.'

Then, just as abruptly, Valentin's tone of voice changed: 'Did you know that Gregor doesn't want to go back to the front? That he wants to head for the forests, like Ursula?' My mother: 'I do know.' Gregor: 'How do you know? Until today I haven't said a word about it.' My mother: 'I know. I knew it. Don't go into the forest. You mustn't join them.' Gregor: 'Why do you avoid the word, Sister? The mere word "partisans", does it make you afraid?' My mother: 'I am neither afraid of the word nor of the partisans themselves. I'm not one of those settled here from Germany, on the farms of those of our people settled in the Reich, I'm not one of those incomers from Iserlohn or from Buxtehude or from wherever, now lodged here, who, at night, when a pumpkin rolls down from the stack in front of the occupied house, crawl under the occupied beds shouting: "Help, the partisans!" And who really start shouting, if snow slides from the roof into the occupied yard, or when, after rain, mine workings cave in and bury the occupied shed: "Bandits! Tito murderers!" But I'm afraid all the same.' Gregor (who is still pushing the pram with 'me' in it back and forward): 'For him there, for my dear godchild? Nothing can happen to him, even someone half-blind like me can see that.' My mother: 'I know nothing can happen to him, for the present. I'm afraid for the rest of us, for our parents, for our property, our—estate, our—land. Strange—I'm not afraid for you either, Gregor.' Gregor: 'Yes, where I'm going now, the fields are called "Beyond Fear".' My mother: 'For our sister to have gone into the forests—the Swabians couldn't give a toss. A woman, from our area, what kind of fighter is she supposed to be, and a farm-maid in clogs at that, in clodhoppers, and to top it all she's short-sighted, and to top it all she's knock-kneed and she constantly stumbles in the kitchen because of it, and what will it be like in the forest? But you, a soldier of the Greater German Reich, who's sworn an oath, joining the partisans—they'll make the rest of us suffer for it, there's nothing else they can do, that is, I don't know, where did I read it, in the Hermagoras Calendar or wherever, the physical law of history. They'll resettle our parents. It almost sounds nice, the word—I resettle, we resettle, we settlers on the settlers' ship on our way to Newfoundland, New Zealand, New Scotland, New Brunswick, New Jaunfeld, Nova Podjuna. But in reality, beyond the words, our parents will be outcasts, displaced persons, herded together in a foreign place where for them there is nothing to settle, never mind land to cultivate, and if there's land to cultivate, to be put in order, then exclusively the fields and factory halls of their lord and lady slave holders in the Spessart Hills, in Teutoburg Forest, in the Black Forest, in the Harz, in the Hunsrück, in the Eifel and in the Giant Mountains. In their huts and round the huts a different forest from yours, one made of signs and every sign a prohibition, and every second prohibition decorated with a death's head, and the main prohibition for our parents in their hut—the ban on speaking their own language, the home and kitchen language, the nature language. Only singing in it will be allowed from time to time, on Sundays, together with the other resettlers, on the round sunny space in the middle of all the homely settler huts. But it will be a song such as only people sing who know that they will never go home again.'

Gregor, after a silence: 'But that's why I'm going into the forests. So that, one day, there will be a homecoming for all our people.' My mother: 'What are you talking about—our parents are at home. Only if you choose the forest—' Gregor: 'And apart from that I've already burnt my uniform.' My mother: 'So what? There are others waiting in the stores, as many as you want.'

Silence again. Then Valentin begins to speak: 'There are rumours going round, according to which something very special is in store for some of our people, for example, those who slaughter a pig for the partisans or just leave a loaf of bread for them. People like that are not resettled, so it's said. Apparently they remain in the country and work off their punishment here, in camps. These camps are supposed to consist mainly of well-ventilated workshops and factory halls, day and night smoking chimneys, as we know them from the English industrial districts—that is, as I know them, don't ask me how. In the opinion of some, munitions are produced there—a secret weapon against Russia or Godknowswho, a kind of Goethe and Schiller organ against the Stalin organ. But the majority opinion is that the camps are primarily engaged in production for peaceful purposes. Thanks to such work, so it is said, the campers are prepared for the coming world peace and released into freedom as transformed persons. Only, no one has yet returned from these reform institutions. Apparently there are many fatalities, even if they are due to natural causes, heart failure, cardiac arrest, not least among our people, with their strong mountaineers' hearts. The letters from the camps, admittedly, paint a different picture—fresh air, good sleep, dreams of paradise, the neighbours more neighbourly than those at home. Also the little bits and pieces which are smuggled outside point, rather, to conditions being good. Mostly these are handkerchiefs, pure white, lovingly embroidered by the people in the camps themselves, our fellows must have learnt to embroider in there!, and what is it that they embroider, on the little bits of cloth?—nothing but cheerful things: the laughing sun, little stars, little flowers at all four corners, cowslips, a house, hearts with little arrows in them, apples, pears, grapes, horse-heal, a football—and the fellows even embroider words, no secret messages but a name, their own, and with it, as on tree trunks, perhaps a girl's name as well, sometimes even several! These cloths are said to be thin, very thin, and small, very small, and the words are apparently even thinner, often hard to read, because the thread again and again runs out and the letters have got mixed up. The likely reason—they are embroidered in pitch darkness, and the man who reported all that to me and is by nature a pessimist, says: "These embroiderers, they always sit, each one alone, in a death cell, and embroidering in pitch darkness is granted them on the night before their execution—and whenever the embroidered cloth comes to light, it's a sign for the family: our son, our brother, our father—and for the sweetheart or sweethearts: my dearest, our dearest—is no longer alive, he has been hanged and buried in a nameless grave for betraying people and race." And look, here is such an embroidered cloth, clothlet—' He at once waves the thing in front of the faces of his two siblings and draws it past them, also past the pram with 'me' in it, and finally draws it across the face of his elder brother: 'The spot of blood there doesn't mean anything, Gregor—the embroiderer concerned pricked his finger while he was embroidering.'

Again unnoticed by the rest of us, another figure must have come onto the scene, perhaps already some time before. We only become aware of her, as a voice bursts out and our heads shoot round as one. A woman is standing there in the half-shadow at the edge of the field, in an army coat and leather boots; on her head, pulled down onto her face, the very cap with the very five-pointed star. Now her voice becomes loud: 'Don't let Valentin talk you round,

Gregor! He doesn't deserve his name—the Strong? No, the weakling, who tells stories. Our family will not be resettled. House and farm remain ours! Our land here will be our land as it never was before! The death cell, that will be for the others, and not even a cell—a spot of urine in the blackberry thorns at the edge of the three-hundred-foot-deep hole in the karst, and with one kick down into the foiba! "I was only a cook," "I was only with the supply troop!" is what they will have whined beforehand, and then, falling, "Mummy-y-y . . .".'

As she was speaking she stepped out of the shadow, and from her three siblings there now comes one after the other: 'Sister. . .', and then from her brother Valentin, in an American accent: 'The farm-maid as commander. The village bumpkin as brigadier.' Thereupon she, in an unexpectedly gentle voice: 'Well observed, Brother. And that—the maid who gives the orders—is exactly how it is. But for now, until the end of the war, don't call me by given name any more. I am no longer Ursula. In the Osvobodilna fronta I have a new name.' Gregor: 'O-svo-bo-dil-na fron-ta, what does that mean?' She: 'Liberation Front. Don't you understand your own language any more?' He: 'Sure. But only when it expresses what one can see, hear and smell. When it becomes general I don't understand it any more. In our language, there is originally nothing general, is there, nothing at all, and for me that's still true today.' She: 'You still have to learn the uses of abstract language, Gregor. You will learn—without the abstractions, the struggle lacks cohesion. Without doctrine, no common goal. Without organization, no superstructure, and without an order of battle—out in the cold. Without literature, no base—will, woods and weapons alone are not enough.'

Gregor: 'What do you mean by literature, Sister? The poems of
France Prešeren, the novels of Ivan Cankar, the "Wild Growths"
of Prežihov Voranc?' She: 'Nonsense! Verse and novels are no literature for fighting troops. There is a time to weep and become
soft with beautiful verses, and there is a time to become hard and
to fall in line thanks to a tougher language. There is a time for mystery and there is a time for plain speaking. Literature, now that
means pamphlets, leaflets, newspapers, manifestos. Such printed
matter is our other weapon. Without it we would be no more than
an isolated troop in the freezing mountain forest. How we thirst
after such literature! The printing presses which our English allies
drop, along with the grenades and the rifles, are part of our arse-
nal—even if on printing the special, the decisive! . . . letters are
missing . . . Not until we had the literature was the group welded
together. The British have recently been dropping printing presses
from which the main part is missing . . . And we can't expect anything for our literature, here in this land, from the other allies
beyond the Karawanks, or at most in Cyrillic letters, which the
people here can't read . . . Despite that we're going to win, Gregor,
zmagala bova . . . we two, as true as in the language of both of us
there exists the dual, bova . . . isn't that so, Gregor? And so you,
too, will now rename yourself and take a name for the struggle.
No Gregor any more, no Svinec any more—only a single name
for the struggle and as cover.' Gregor: 'First, reveal your own,
Madame Commissar.' She, in an unexpectedly gentle voice: 'I
thought about it for a long time. As what could I rebaptize myself?
At that time I still loved the snow, the sneg—now, in the mountain
forests, less so. And so I was given the name Snežena, Snowy. And
the rebaptism, it gave me strength. The new name—it changed me

into someone I secretly always have been. And now you!' Gregor: 'Right here and now!' Snežena: 'Yes, on the spot.' Gregor: 'I don't want a new name. I'm Gregor. Must there be a new name?' Snežena: 'There must. Otherwise you won't be considered for the Resistance. And you do want that, don't you?' Gregor: 'It's the only way. But as for me. Which resistance? What kind?' Snežena: 'Only one is possible now. The forest future. Kill or be killed. Yes, you will have to kill, Gregor. And this is now the last time that the world has heard your peacetime name—"Gregor", "the awakened, the watchful". Find a name with "war" or "death"!' He: 'Not with "death"!' Snežena: 'Well, then any name—only you must rebaptize yourself! You'll see, the new name will turn you inside out, as it turned me inside out. It will help you to your feet, you will stand there transformed, finally on solid ground, and not so unsteadily as with your eternal apples and pears under you. And at the same time it'll grab you, for another star.' He: 'I can't. Another name, it's not right. A bolt of lightning will strike me for it, from the heavens or wherever.' Snežena: 'So then I will just be your rebaptizer. And now you will finally stop pushing the pram with him in it back and forward.' (Did he obey?) 'So: From today your name is Jonatan—like one of your apple varieties. And, in accordance with it, you will become active!' Gregor-Jonatan, after a moment of silence: 'Apple activist.' And after a further silence I hear Valentin say: 'Mystery of faith. I would have preferred "Cox", it comes from England, or, even better, "Ontario", it comes from America . . .'

I on my bench in the middle of the steppe-like heath could then hardly believe my ears: Following the renaming, Snežena literally addressed her newly baptized brother in a speech: 'Now you stand on the good side of history, Comrade Jonatan. We are at war with a great web of violence and of hate. In the end, history will prove us right. It's history that decides. It speaks the truth. History is the highest, the final, the irrevocable judge. We fighters in the forests, in the Karawanks and on the Svinjska planina, we are its vanguard and its heralds. We are a young troop, many of us are still almost children. But, in accordance with the Holy Scriptures, the time has come to put away childish things. Our people will play the part in history that befits it. Until now we were strangely exempt, and yet we were a race of rebels. And now we are here to point the way. It is time to choose the path of history. It is time to shake and rattle at everything in order to found our land anew, following the example of our forefathers, who saw the land as more than the sum of mere individual ambitions. Our eyes fixed on the horizon, let us confront the adverse winds. We are the patrols of freedom, and our people is the one God has called on to seek after the new life. And in it we will hold out our hands to our haters—if they are ready to open their fists.'

In glancing over my shoulder, while sporadically making notes, I observed that she herself had clenched her fist—both fists, and that Gregor-Jonatan stared at them, transfixed. Ursula-Snežena signals to him to follow her and walks away. He follows her at first, then, however, goes in another direction. She: 'Where are you going? That's not the way.' Jonatan: 'I know. But first I want to make a detour.' Snežena: 'Not a long one, I hope.' He says nothing. She: 'Leave your pruning shears here. In the forests there is nowhere a fruit tree to trim.' Jonatan: 'Who knows. Till later then, Sister.' And, circling, he disappears from the scene.

At a shout from my mother (who has now taken over the pushing of the pram), the snowy one, for her part, pauses before leaving. 'Hey, Sister.' And the 'Commissar' does indeed turn with a sister face. And now my mother: 'Who is it that washes the washing in the forest, who sews and patches, who cooks?' Snežena: 'The women, the girls, Jelka, Andrina, Javora, Milena . . .' My mother: 'And you?' Snežena: 'I do, too, and I polish the men's shoes, and I carry supplies up the mountain and I do my share of night-time sentry duty. That's how it's conceived. That's how it has worked out. Farewell, Sister. Srečno. With luck . . .'

She's gone. Valentin and my mother are now alone, with me, at a distance. My mother: 'What strangers the people from the next village can become. To say nothing of the neighbours. And strangers more than all the rest one's own folk, parents, brothers and sisters.' Valentin, pointing at the pram: 'And? Motherly love?' My mother: 'Sometimes less, sometimes more. Sometimes happiness, sad, very sad happiness. Then sometimes he is so alien to me, that I would like to thrash him, thrash his infant arse with a piece of wood. Tip him, who sucks me dry, into the nettles together with the pram. I alone am not enough for him. He also needs his father. I have to go and look for him, out in the Reich, or wherever.' Valentin: 'And you? Do you need the man?' My mother: 'No. Not any more.' Valentin (am I hearing right?): 'You've betrayed me, Sister, with another! And what another! If at least it had been an Apache or a Navajo or an Athabascan.' My mother: 'I know. In the beginning I did feel guilty. Later, not any more.'

And again the taciturnity of our clan. Then I hear my mother: 'Let us go home now, Valentin, home to our parents. Since Benjamin is no longer with us, they hardly talk to each other. From morning to night, each person in the house stares into a different corner. And the young pup there doesn't cheer them up, far from it. "What on earth has he got to laugh at so silently?" asks our mother. "Why on earth does he keep staring up at the ceiling?" asks our father.' Thereupon Valentin: 'No, I'm not going home. Because my presence will confront our parents on every day of my leave with the fact that I, the dodgy son, am alive and that he, their darling, is dead.' (He has shifted to a kind of singing meanwhile, a kind not at all Jaunfeld-like.) 'No, I'm not going home, because when I step inside there I'm even less than nobody. No, I'm not going into the forest because it's dark in the forest and my dark sister lurks there. I'll go to the next village, to Milka with the yellow ribbon in her hair, and then to the next village, to Lena with the white breast, and then to the next one, to Angelika with the mouse in her straw mattress. And then? And then? Home to the foreign war . . .'

So brother and sister go off in different directions, and, as they disappear, I hear from her or from him: 'How one gets pushed around . . .', and as an echo: 'Yes, how one gets pushed around. Instead of us being able to sit down here together again in a manner pleasing to God.' And as echo: 'Sit down together in a manner pleasing to God—that is what being active means. That is politics!'

four

And again I'm sitting alone on the bench on the steppe-like heath of the Jaunfeld. Gusts of wind, rustling of dry leaves, tinkling of bare branches as in an ice wind, ravens, tits, cuckoo calls—like all the seasons in one. And once again I will have tried to speak plainly and once again now getting muddled, now beginning to stutter, repeatedly breaking off, taking back what's been said, casting doubt and so on: 'On more or less the same day on which one of my mother's brothers, instead of returning to the world war after his leave, joined the partisans in the forests of the Svinjska planina, and a few days before the other surviving brother reported back to the ice front, there was announced, on twentieth August nineteen forty-three, the solemn Moscow Declaration, in which the Austrians were called on to offer armed resistance to the enforced community with the German Reich. Such resistance, it was stated, was the condition of the recognition of Austrian independence after the war. In the land, some isolated individuals followed the call but they remained isolated. They wanted to resist, it's true, but knew neither how nor where nor when. Only a few found their way here, to Carinthia, where the resisters of the Slovenian minority had given themselves a military organization. A mistake to think that the few from other regions who joined the partisans were motivated by party politics, for example, the members of the banned

Austrian Communist Party. It continued to exist underground, but, despite the Moscow Declaration, its leadership came out against an armed struggle, on the grounds that there were so few secret party members that, if these were to take up arms, there was a risk that, by the end of the war, the Communist Party of Austria would have no members. Instead, the few German-speaking countrymen who joined the Slovenian partisan units in Carinthia were deserters, also railway workers and, in addition to those, one or other loner, as one would say today: a wayside shrine painter from east Tyrol, a Jew's harp player from Upper Austria, a former competitive skier from the Pinzgau in Salzburg land, a shepherd from the Montafon. And the struggle, with or without the Moscow Declaration, really got going from autumn nineteen forty-three—because of the reinforcements that had stumbled here into our land and our Jaunfeld from the rest of Austria? God alone knows. At any rate, here in autumn and winter and in the following year, there took place the only battles within the borders of the Thousand Year Reich involving resisters to it. The resistance army was commanded exclusively by former woodcutters, farm labourers, sawmill workers, journeymen millers. A mistake, again, to assume that, among the leaders, there were members of the local educated class, teachers, lawyers, doctors. At most, a couple of priests, for whom saving their own language was part of the practice of religion—saving language is saving souls—secretly supported the fight of their lambs, or whatever they were, and that one or other clergyman who even held Mass for those now all the more fervently in need of the Word of God, indeed were thirsting after it, did so with a sub-machine gun leaning against the open-air altar. The members, how can I put it, of the local upper stratum, those with education, as they're called, were absent throughout the time of the great and only resistance in this country and they remained absent to the end. Their absence wasn't exactly condoned by the farm labourers, it was lamented again and again, when, speechless among themselves, they didn't know how to go on. "Our educated people, where are they, when we need them? The people can hardly wait for words from us. But we, what do we have to say? The gentlemen don't care about our folk. Our scholars, they're saving themselves for better times. But we, and the people, we need them as spokesmen, to point the way. It's not enough to load weapons, to add wood to the fire, to make coffee. In accordance with the saying that there are some who look after the cattle and others who look after the words and that both together look after house and farm . . ." '

In time, with so much plain speaking, my tongue has grown heavy. A weariness has come over me, and I have slipped from the bench in the middle of the Jaunfeld to the foot of the apple tree. I rest now in its root hollow, as if sleeping and at the same time in anticipation of what happens next. And what happens next? My grandparents approach, each from a different direction. Both, not yet really old, are dressed in blue country working clothes. My grandfather is pulling a short, broad, almost rectangular boat behind him, my grandmother a full handcart with two big milk churns on it. Wordlessly they leave boat and cart standing and sit down on the bench, right beside me, as if I wasn't there at all. Then he: 'And?' My grandmother: 'Nothing.' My grandfather: 'No forces' letter from Valentin since last summer. No sign from Gregor, although he's supposedly looking down on us the whole time from up there in the forest. And no news from Ursula.' My grandmother:

'It wouldn't be from her personally. Better no news at all.' The father: 'Letters at best from our other daughter. That she's still looking out there in Greater Germany for her all-German to go with her half-German child.' The mother: 'How beautiful her handwriting is. So school was good for something, at least.' The father: 'Only, from one letter to the next ever fewer words in our own language.' The mother: 'Hm.' The father: 'Hm.' And then the father, pointing at the churns: 'How many litres?' The mother: 'Twenty-two and a half.' The father: 'Yesterday they still gave twenty-six. Add some water before you deliver the milk to the Swabians.' The mother: 'Lead me not into temptation. And the lake?' The father: 'Full of leeches. They're already waiting. It can't come too soon for them.' Both in chorus: 'Hm.'

Suddenly a figure approaches the pair. No one saw him coming. It is as if he had grown out of the heathland soil. Perhaps also because of the coat, a long one, its colour merging with the surroundings. As he comes closer, turning full circle and occasionally even going backwards, he could be some stroller. But the gun he's holding and the blackened face hardly fit with that—only now, as the figure comes to a stop in front of the grandparents, do the contours become clear. 'Who goes there?' exclaims my grandfather, as if he himself were still in the war, the first one, and then: 'Kdo si? Who are you?' His wife beside him already seems to have known for some time but she only laughs silently, whereupon the figure picks an apple from the little tree and holds it out, whereupon the grandfather only says the name of his son: 'Gregor!' and the mother: 'Jonatan.'

Gregor-Jonatan joins his parents, sitting down on the edge of the boat or wherever. As he does so, it is revealed that he is wearing a uniform under his coat, not a German one, and has a rucksack on his back, a noticeably empty one. He wipes the soot from his face. The three look at one another for a while without saying anything. Then the mother speaks: 'You must be hungry.' Jonatan: 'Half the time up there in the forest we only talk about food. Leg of lamb roasted in bacon, have mercy on us. Crumbed buckwheat tossed in dripping with crackling, hear us. Veal sausages with sauerkraut, have mercy on us. Boiled beef with horseradish sauce, hear us. Smoked venison ham with juniper berries, have mercy on us. Pancakes stuffed with cranberry jam, bring peace to our stomachs.' The mother: 'Here in this can'—she picks up a smaller can from between the large ones—'is goat's milk, from the unregistered goat—' Jonatan: '—which likes best of all to eat the clematis blossom. What milk that is, Mother! Thanks to it we shall yet be in paradise today, for the time it takes to wipe one's mouth.' And already he has stowed away the can in his rucksack. Turning round the father has conjured up from the boat's stern a bundle of fish, freshly caught, so it appears, trout or pike perch or whatever, and wordlessly held it out to his son who once again packs away the treasure in the twinkling of an eye, and then speaks: 'Our cook will roast the fish today, in a fire such as only he can make, without flying sparks and without smoke that betrays us, with brushwood dry as straw, which he alone fetches.' The father: 'Years ago, I would cut you children short every time you said "I", do you still remember?' Jonatan: 'How could I forget, Father? "There'll be no I in this house!" And although in our dear language there is normally no separate word for "I"—"I" am hidden in the ending of the verb, is what we learnt in the school in Maribor, gled*am*, "I look", ljub*im*, "I love"—back then at home and in the farmyard you even wanted to drive the hidden I-form out of us, no "I feel", no "I think", no "I would like", to say nothing of the emphatic "*I* say", "*I* think", "jaz menim", "jaz mislim" . . . "In our house there is room only for we and us!" is what you said . . .' The father: 'As a forced soldier with them you said "I", wrote "I", sang "I"—even emphasized the "I"! But now, up there in the forests, it seems to me—' Jonatan: 'Yes, Father. Among us fighters, the word "I" has been deleted from our vocabulary.' The mother: 'My Gregor a fighter?' Jonatan: 'Yes, Mother. We long for battle, for open battle. We have already been lying hidden for far too long.' And he strokes and pats his gun as he speaks, and even embraces it? The father: 'And when will you finally attack?' Jonatan: 'We lack heavy weapons—the British drop almost all of them over hostile territory, on the plains. And the Swabians are waiting for us there with the most modern British machine guns . . .' He stands up to leave. The father: 'How impressively you stand there! When I think how all of us here on our Jaunfeld, whether woman or man, out of old habit are forever shifting from one foot to the other—' He demonstrates it—'and how back then, during the First World War, from the Italian Front to Galicia, I was absolutely unable to rid myself of the habit . . . and how in every village between the Saualpe and the Karawanks there is at least one place with the name "Fidget's Farm" . . .' Jonatan, after a silence: 'Do you know, Parents, that when we look down from the mountains onto the Jaunfeld, we've given each of the farms, where we know our families are, a secret name, different from the one in the land register? That's part of being . . . underground, Mother . . . For example, "Back Fence

Farm", "Back Garden Farm", "Cockroach Farm", "Hammer Farm", "Glowing Stove Farm", "Chamois Farm", "Boxtree Farm", "Flail Farm", "Deadly Nightshade Farm", "Cowslip Farm", "Trembler Farm" ' The mother: 'That would be well-matched with us—' Jonatan: 'We're called something different.' And his voice assumes a mock whisper: 'Do you want to know what our farm is called by the fighters in the forest? "Pri Zavadnem. A—" ' The mother whispers too: ' "Aware Farm"?' Jonatan: 'Yes, "Aware Farm"!' The father, loud: 'And what do you do with the other half of your time, apart from remaining hidden?' Jonatan: 'We plan the peace—apart from when the lice torment us too much.' The father: 'So you believe in your victory?' Jonatan: 'Nothing else can happen.' The father: 'Why?' Jonatan: 'That's what history demands. And history is the victorious power.' The father: 'Now even you are boasting about history, Gregor—' Jonatan: 'Jonatan . . .' The father: 'In our house—no history! "Aware Farm" doesn't fit our house. Let its inherited name be.' Jonatan: 'Leadworker Farm?' The father: 'Leadworker Farm.' Jonatan: 'Your house isn't up there in the forest, Father. There you don't have any say.' The mother: 'And what will the peace be like?' Jonatan: 'We will no longer be the unwanted and cursed outsiders in the land between the Karawanks and the Svinjska planina. No one will call us "obstinate Slavs" again. Here we've always been at the bottom of the pile, under the Monarchy, then in the Republic, then in the Corporative State and more than ever now in the Thousand Year Reich.' The father: 'And after the war, we last shall be the first?' Jonatan: 'At any rate, this land will at last also be our land, for the first time in—history, dear Parents.' At that the parents only looked silently at each other. And then I hear the mother again: 'Have you heard anything about your sister?' Jonatan: 'No. And besides, for us all the women who fight with us are sisters. That's also how we address them, and to the man next to me in the forest I say brother.' The father: 'What a language you speak, Son. No one in our clan has ever spoken in that way before.' The mother: 'Just let him be, Father. You've never been able to let your children be.' Jonatan has meanwhile turned to leave. In doing so he has stepped over me, lying at the foot of the little tree, has briefly bent down and whispered in my ear: 'Take note and don't forget! Go on dreaming, little dreamer. At least that can't do any harm, unlike most other activities today, a good and bad half century after the here and now. Ah, Chief Morning Breeze!' And then as suddenly as he had appeared he is gone again and has left his parents, my grandparents, alone on the bench on the steppe-like heath. It should be added here that, shortly before, who knows when, a single apple went from hand to hand and each person took a bite from it, in accordance with the words: 'This do in remembrance of me.' And it seems to me now that the sentence could also be clearly heard.

Time has passed, I no longer know how. It has become neither dark nor bright. Nor have any particular sounds indicated a passing of time. But it has passed, time. My grandparents have remained sitting without moving. It almost appears to me now that they were paralysed or, rather, absorbed, each in their own thoughts. Perhaps they have also closed their eyes. And the wind has perhaps changed direction? Yes, that's how it will have been. And after a while they will both have opened their eyes again. The wind is cold. My grandmother appears to be shivering. Her husband rubs her hands. Then I hear her: 'They have burnt our bee house with a flamethrower. They hung the child of a neighbour head-down from a plum tree. They slit open the stomach of one our people and defiled the corpse.' He: 'You've dreamt that, Mother.' She: 'Some of it yes, some of it no.' He: 'They have forced us to write our names differently. They have Germanized our beautiful names!' She: 'You've dreamt that, Father.' He: 'Just imagine—not "Svinec", s-v-i-n-e-c any more—no, now we have to sign ourselves "Swinetz" or face a heavy punishment! Just imagine—w instead of v, and instead of the c at the end a tz. Double u, tee, zed, is that not dreadful? Tee, zed, tee, zed—first the Huns, then the Turks, and now the Swabians, these three. But worst of all are the Germans!' She: 'Let them be.' He: 'You always want to let the others be, Mother. You're always conciliatory. You always want to see the best in everyone. Every word a gospel. Small wonder that we don't get anywhere with all the let-it-be lead in our shoes.' And she: 'The good old days—they did exist, here in our Jaunfeld, at least. They did exist, because we experienced them.' And he: 'Yes, they were no illusion.'

And again suddenly, as if grown out of the ground or fallen from the sky—without a sound of anything falling—now their daughter Ursula, war name Snežena, is standing in front of them and of me lying on the ground. Unlike her brother she is not camouflaged, so that Father and Mother recognize her immediately. Father: 'Mojdunaj, Ursula!', and the mother: 'Madonna, Mother of God! Let's take a look at you! Snežena!' And the latter lets them take a good look. A suggestion of the familiar clan wail of joy—already over. Snežena walks in a circle round parents, handcart, boat, tree and me curled up there. Under her coat, which is perhaps no more than a camouflage cloth (in the snow), she, too, is in military dress. But her bearing no longer accords with that, nor does her voice: 'Locked into the smokehouse . . . all night long his weeping and shouting . . . "Let me live, in my mother's name!" . . . "Help! Help!" . . . Never was a night so long . . . In the morning I went down on my knees in front of the Commandant and begged with folded hands for Sergej to be reprieved . . . But he was unmoved . . . "Offences against partisan discipline must be punished by death!" . . . And all that for a stolen lump of butter . . . "It's not the first time he has shown himself unworthy of our liberation front—he already once fell asleep on sentry duty!" . . . I could understand the bit about discipline, but that partisans—execute one of their own! Despite everything he was with us, was for us, in the Resistance . . . to shoot him because he had kept a little piece of butter for himself . . . As the detail was taking him away, I stood in front of them and shouted: "Children, what are you doing?" . . . But everyone looked through me and most of all the Commandant—even Sergej, he admittedly with huge eyes—what is it we say? "Fear has big eyes" . . . And when the detail returned without him, one said: "Sad—but that's just how it is in war, there's nothing else to be done, it has to be," and another of the squad said: "And anyway, when all his begging did no good, in his last moments he wished the enemy on us: 'The Germans will avenge me! Let the Swabians kill you all. All of you!' " Yet, I'm sure Sergej only made a pretence of cursing us—because, what is it people say? "Fear puts on an act, but not a good one" . . . And do you know who executed him? Had him executed? Who was the commander? Who is our commandant? Guess. No, don't guess. You'll regret it, if you do guess who it is.' (Pauses in her circling movement) 'I've realized this now, Parents—wherever killing is done, no matter how, that's not where I belong. That's not my world. For me there is no world at all, I don't belong anywhere, except in the farmyard, with the cows and pigs. I always only talked about killing. Just as in our clan we constantly talk about killing—"I'm going to kill him!", "I'm going to strike them dead!"—and are never ever killers. I'm no good for fighting. We're no good for fighting, no matter which. At most we rise up once, now and then. But the true struggle, a lasting struggle has no future with us.' (She resumes her circling.) 'But what does have a future? What on earth?' The mother, then, at some point: 'Up there in the skies, the Wild Hunt will race past, and we, instead of sheltering from it as usual, instead of lying down together on the ground and forming a wheel, will remain standing upright and greet the squadron: "Be even wilder! Even more evil!" In the night, when we're sleeping, Trota Mora will squat on us, and instead of getting no more air to breathe as usual we will heave a sigh of relief under her weight and sing: "Trota Mora, make yourself heavier! Even heavier!" And each time another one of us is lying in the grave, we will say: "There he lies, out of sight." For now there's no way back to the farmyard, Snežena. Either-Or. Either continue, as if nothing had happened, or—no or. Only the either. March, back into the mountains.' Snežena: 'What do you have that I can take with me?' And like her brother she holds out an empty rucksack to her parents, which is filled by her father and mother from boat and handcart, accompanied by a litany which all three take turns in saying: 'Crayfish.' 'Apple strudel.' 'Potatoes, unfortunately already sprouting.' 'Smoked meat, from our own smoke room.' 'Guglhupf, with cinnamon, raisins and nuts.' 'Eggs.' 'Butter . . . here . . .' 'Quinces, against the lice.' 'Ceps.' —'Not them, there's more than enough of

them in the forests, and no one picks them. Fungi and fighters, they
don't go together.' And, to take her leave, Snežena has joined her
parents on the bench and got what she has to tell all muddled up:
'We eat, if at all, only once a day . . . Our bunker is a bark hut,
such as only the woodcutters of Carinthia can put up . . . When I
sing our partisan songs, I have a rosary in my fingers at the same
time . . . We have several typewriters but no one can type . . .
Through the telescope the Germans can be recognized by their
broad belts with "God with us" on them . . . Sometimes we are so
tired that only laughing keeps us on our feet . . . Among ourselves
we identify each other by passwords, for example, "The plums are
ripe". "But it's not autumn yet" . . . The farmer at "Boxtree Farm"
does the most to support us, only he can't manage the word "partisans", he always says "p-p-artisans" . . . And in spring I once
saw little lillies in the tall grass of a clearing and thought:
"Mother!" . . .' And then she, too, turns to leave, with a full rucksack. 'At times in the forest I longed to see my sister's child—
strange. To see the little monster with his foreign look, his little
salamander hands, his hair which smells like wet chicken feathers,
his skin, on which, even after weaning, one still smells the mother's
milk. As if after everything that has taken place only the sight of
an innocent child could cleanse one, even the sight of one, who
already on the day of his birth did not seem so innocent at all . . .'
I raised my head to attract her attention. But she has already disappeared, as suddenly as she came. The father, or whoever, called
after her into the darkness, whether she had heard anything about
her brother. And Snežena called back out of the darkness, that he
had risen from courier to commandant! He was called "the Dis-
armer", because, with his battalion he managed to disarm whole

enemy units, without even a single round of ammunition being wasted. And the mother, or whoever, had called after her: 'And love? Awakened at last, by the war?' And, already far off, Snežena's shouted reply: 'Love is something immature, and, apart from that, it doesn't lead anywhere.'

And again, with my grandparents on the bench in the middle of the Jaunfeld, and myself at the roots of the tree, time has passed. The wind has turned once more and come vertically from above, a downhill wind, like the San Andreas wind sometimes in the desert, down onto the little tree alone, which was slightly compressed by it. The pair on the bench have hardly been touched. Have they heard the sighing at all? And again a letter, blown there by the San Andreas wind. And again it's my grandfather who opens it. And it is now he who says: 'I knew it.' His wife takes the letter out of his hand and reads aloud: '. . . his young life for the Führer and our great Djerman Fatterland . . .' Both in chorus: 'Valentin.' And thereupon likewise in unison a sound almost like a snort— and silence. Then the father, or whoever: 'He never wanted to wear short trousers, especially not long underpants, not even in the coldest wind.' The mother, or whoever (for a while both voices, at least to me lying on the ground, sound the same): 'But that was Benjamin. Valentin was against braces. Absolutely no braces! Either nothing, or a belt! The girls like lads with belts, best of all with a bronze buckle and a tongue that hangs down a little at the hip. Meet a girl and you're wearing braces then you've had it from the word go.' The father, or whoever: 'And his handwriting, sometimes slanting to the left, sometimes to the right, sometimes tiny, sometimes huge—different every day.' The mother, or whoever: 'And the curve of his fingernails.' The father, or whoever: 'And the little iron tips on his Sunday shoes.' And again the parents were silent for a while. And then I clearly hear the mother: 'When those of us, who on the soil of the Reich—which was once our very own soil here—are regarded by the chiefs of the Reich as enemies of the Reich, are then forced to stand in front of them, the chiefs, then it is, as you know, Father, forbidden for our people to look them, the Reich chiefs in the eye, excepting the case, that one of our children has sacrificed his life on the battlefield or wherever for their Reich, whereupon, as you know, Father, the Reich chief, before he reads out to our people the sad news, which is at the same time supposed to make one proud, commands our people: "Eyes up!", which for our people is the one and only opportunity and one and only privilege, to be allowed to look the chief in his Greater German eyes— do you understand?' The father: 'Hm. In my whole life I've never heard such a long sentence from you, Mother.' The mother: 'So: Eyes up!' And by craning and stretching I can see that my grandparents have stood up—and their eyes? up, up! far above anyone's eye level, even that of a giant. And so I hear them spitting skywards together—weakly and ever more weakly, since the one as well as the other lacks spittle. And then the mother: 'They should know that we are their enemies!' And then the father: 'Again someone fallen into despair. "Well, well!" says the Dear Lord. Ah, if only our Gregor would be killed as well, and our Ursula, and the other with her little monster, under the bombs, out there, in her German Reich. Then at least we would be all alone here.' And thereupon the mother: 'You're blaspheming.' And thereupon the father: 'Yes. Yes!' And thereupon the mother: 'Go on blaspheming! Blaspheme. Blaspheme for me.'

Now Gregor-Jonatan approaches. He comes without camouflage, noisily—without any conspiratorial behaviour—an (almost) complete disregard. He also looks ragged, without a weapon, in his grey-white linen cloth—or parachute coat—not unlike someone playing a ghost. And that is how he now speaks, after the 'Let's take a look at you!' of his parents, without any preliminary: 'Seen right—I'm no more than a ghost now. Mountain ghosts all of us. There are so many of them down in the valleys. Hardly any of us believes in victory any more. They introduced more and more false resisters into our groups who play partisans and in truth betray us, our camps, our bunkers. These ragged devils speak our language, they come from our people and yet are the henchmen of the master race which can stay genteelly in the background and wash its hands and plead ignorance, as everywhere in Europe, from Oradour to Ukraine. Ragged devils, raztrganci, dividing us, disguised as pickers of mushrooms and of mountain-meadow herbs with salt for the game in their rucksacks. What's the saying: "Snakes that hide their legs"? Only once did one betray himself, "I am a partisan!" he introduced himself, with a German *s* instead of a Slav "partizan"— we've got you! Hung by the feet from a mountain-meadow pine, his head in an ant heap . . .' The father, or whoever, interrupts him: 'How do you know that? Were you there? Did you in the end—?' Jonatan: 'Someone told me.' The mother or whoever: 'People tell so many things nowadays . . .' Jonatan continues: 'We are so few up there against the superior strength below and every day we lose someone. And we can't even bury our dead. Fleeing, fleeing, fleeing, through the day, through the nights. Waiting for our allies? No one is still waiting for covering fire from the British. And our guardian angels? It's true they arrange rendezvous with us but, as in the folk song, not until the hour of our death, and, as in the folk song, they prolong at most the dying and don't provide even a breath of comfort. There they lie then, the dying, in the snow, and all we can do is put a handful of snow on their lips, so that at least they're not thirsty when death comes. How I used to love the snow once. And how repellent it has become to me now, when it falls and when it lies and on the night marches we sink into it up to our necks. One man always in the footprints of the one in front, so that it looks as if only one man has passed that way. And, in the places where there are no trees, the last in line obliterating the tracks with a branch. Almost relaxation to walk on the firm snow of an avalanche, because there one doesn't sink in and leaves hardly a trace. Except the damned Saualpe is far too gentle for good avalanches. And how repellent I now find our much celebrated Drava, naša Drava. Silently it flows, according to the folk song once again, through our land here, isn't it so, unlike the lively Sava on the other side of the Karawanks. But no! It's only cold and its water dirty, and deep, and as a non-swimmer—all of us partisans are non-swimmers—I almost drowned one night when I wanted to cross in a boat like that one, we made it ourselves, more like a barrel, in order at last to re-establish contact, an absolute essential, between us scattered partisans on this side and the other side. Do you know what I think when I see your boat, Father? Coffin. And when I think of the Drava? Grave—and by no means a holy one. I regard it as my enemy when I see it from above, winding gently in the sun through our land. Damned Drava. Accursed snow. On the night marches I fall asleep again and again, my eyes open, and fall onto the man in front who in turn falls onto the man in front. On the brink of despair, it was, each time, almost a miracle when someone in the column began a song, one born from the brink of despair, it didn't matter which, it didn't have to be a resistance song, perhaps just "Does a Star in the Foreign Land Know Me . . .", and strength returned. Except by now no one sings on the marches through the snow any more. At most someone clears his throat, or curses, and one of the mules brays. I drag myself along, let myself be dragged along, like a dead man. It used to be that, while we were marching, the word was passed from one man to the next: "Are you still close to the man in front? Keep contact to the man in front!" But no one says even that any more. Mutely we stagger all night long, I stagger uphill and downhill, indifferent to any kind of contact.' He pauses. 'Contact is contact, isn't it? The main thing is that the word still exists, isn't it? Strange, how what I merely thought to myself has become dubious when I spoke it out loud . . . And have you noticed, Father, how I've been saying "I" more and more often? And strange again, how the pictures of us as ghosts, as dead men, as scattered, have looked different to me from picture to picture, from word to word, and not any more like ghosts, half-dead, isolated—the opposite? no!—something else . . . Shall I give myself up? What should I do?' The father: 'Stay with us, Gregor. No one will look for you here. Our house isn't being watched any more, since Benjamin—and not at all now, since—you are our last son.' He hands his son the forces' letter with the second death notice. Jonatan reads. No movement. Silence. The father then continues: 'The farm needs you. Your orchard is waiting for you. It's getting mossy. The branches need to be cut. It's not just the Jonatan Apple and the Good Louise of Avranches that are asking after you. You're an apple man, and an apple man is no good for war.' Jonatan: 'And you, Mother? What do you say? In our clan you were always the only one who knew. The only one who knows.' And his mother? Stands up and fills his rucksack, didn't you see it, with provisions, a whole ham? a pig's head? a plucked turkey? At any rate, the bag contains as much as if it were bottomless. And what does she say then? 'March, back into the snow! Back across the Drava for a second bath.' And Jonatan: 'Where is it written?' And the mother: 'In the Book of Life.' And the son: 'And how does it go on?' And the mother: 'Yes, if I only knew . . . Take a hold of yourself, and go.' And Jonatan has disappeared, after he has taken a hold of himself.

And again time passes, with my grandparents on the bench on the Jaunfeld heath. The wind is now blowing, it seems to me, from all sides, and most forcefully up from below, an upwind, as if from the centre of the earth. The little tree, in whose weave of roots I am lying, is bent upwards together with the remaining apples, and from the fruit there comes a metallic sound, a rattling and clattering. Out of it I hear my grandfather, after a sigh which drowned out the wind: 'How long this war lasts. In the first winter, people said: "The end, or victory, or whatever, is imminent." And now it's already the fifth winter and the final victory supposedly only a matter of time. But which time?' Thereupon my grandmother, after she, too, has sighed our sigh: 'Ah, peace. Nothing as beautiful as peace once was. And in our language as well: "Mir!" ' The man: 'How solemn all the tasks carried out in house and farm are then. The harnessing of the horse—' The woman takes the words out of his mouth: 'The bottling of the raspberries, the blackberries, the blueberries and last in the year then the cranberries, from up on the Svinjska planina—how they shone ruby red . . . and—' The man in turn takes the words out of her mouth: 'And the salting of the sides of bacon fat—' The woman: 'And the treading of the sauerkraut, the pickling of the cucumbers—' The man: 'And the wintering of the turnips in the fields—' The woman: 'And the storing of the apples in the cellar—' The man: 'And our sons and daughters entering the good room—' The woman: 'Holy was peace, holy, holy, holy.' The man: 'Without politics, without emperor, without republic we farmed our farm—' The woman: '—and were our own kings—' The man: '—were the kings of the feast. That's how it was, peace. And where are they now, the kings?' The woman: 'The kings of of peace are dead, they found nothing more to farm.' The man: 'And what will the coming peace be like?' The woman: '—if it comes . . . Sometimes it seems to me that the end of the world has already come. Now everything is only as-if. As if peace came. As if the world existed. As if there were children.' The man: 'And you say that?' The woman: 'And I say that.'

The couple on the bench don't appear to have noticed at all that, in the middle of their stream of words, leaflets or something have fluttered down, a whole swarm of them, across the wide plain. And as I now raise my head and glance around there is, unexpectedly, someone in the background, impossible to say whether a man or a woman, passing by with a ladder, something like an orchard ladder, together with a basket for the picked fruit and a picking bag, serrated at the edges, together with a long pole for 'fishing down'. Admittedly, he quickly disappeared, but he's followed by another figure, with a ball under his arm, followed by yet another, walking along with a bird-cage, in it a dozen brightly coloured birds all mixed up, his path crossed by another figure, taking a huge cat, or whatever it is, to the vet, or wherever, in a kind of woven cage, followed by two chimney sweeps, like father and son, crossed by three anglers, like father, son and grandson. Then another figure with stones in both hands. Is he going to throw them? No, he uses them, round as they are, as skittles bowls. And at the edge of the scene a wrestling match? No, one man is giving the other a leg up. And then a man strolls by, whom an age ago I saw at the side of a country road in countryside Sunday-best clothes, wind blowing his trouser legs, there he goes from age to age. And there, as well, their paths crossing, two with 'peace pipes'. And one, who as he walks is shuffling a pack of cards. And moments of a snowball fight. And apple throwing. And a couple peeling corncobs as they walk . . .

And now, from another background, Gregor-Jonatan appears, 'military' as never before. And he's already talking at the top of his voice, while he's far away, at the same time stroking and patting his gun: 'Živio, Parents, zdravo! Their capitulation is now only a question of time—' His parents in chorus: 'Question of time?' Jonatan: '—of hours, of days, of a week at most. Even their country police, the most poisonous of all, are turning gentle and calling us the liberation army. And the two or three Austrians in our army— yes, we are an army by now!—' The mother or the father: ' "Austrians"?' Jonatan: 'The German-speakers. The two or three Austrians have meanwhile become a whole battalion. And our English allies are again really and truly our allies. They're dropped by parachute and fight with us, die for us here, officers too, especially them. And all the Yugoslav peoples, all have liberated themselves now and are on our side.' (He bends down to me for an impromptu.) 'I know, Godchild, you don't care for generalities. But there are moments when they're the right thing. And you don't need to copy them all down. After the war we will reach out to the people in the land and together we will belong to the great free Europe. No one will be a slave any more in this country, no people will want to oppress another any more. For the first time in our history, we will be free, Parents. Free above all to speak our language. No one will ever bark at us, in the restaurant, on the train, in the bus, in government offices to speak Djerman, if you please, or . . . None of them will ever be in charge in our beloved land, of anything concerning us. Yes, beloved land, here—even when I was at the fruit-tree school over in Slovenia I constantly felt I wanted to go home. And even now during the war, whenever I was on the other side of the Karawanks, I couldn't wait to come home, here to the Svinjska planina, to our language border. Homesickness, everlasting, domo-tožje, od vekomaj do vekomaj. Homesickness for beautiful Carinthia, for lepa Koroška, feminine in our language . . . Do you know, by the way, that there's a first liberated republic? The Free Republic of Zell Pfarre-Sele?' The father and/or the mother: 'But Zell Pfarre is just a village.' Jonatan: 'But a big village, a very big village. And do you know how my unit got a foretaste of the imminent peace? And how I myself got a premonition of it?' (And again he bends down to me.) 'Now this is something to write down, Godchild. There was once that I finally got a quiet sleep there in the mountain forest. All the months before, from night march to night march, we always had to sleep on the steep slopes—if it was possible to sleep at all. We braced our feet against the trees, otherwise in our half-dead sleep we would have plunged down head over heels. Night after night that was all that preoccupied us. And again and again some of us did slip down and then fall, luckily, usually, into a thicket, me too. But recently there have been no more night marches, we no longer flee before them. And I have found my hollow to sleep in. It's lined with ferns and fir twigs and a chamois skin is spread over that, no, several skins! And a chamois skin as a blanket as well—if you down here in the lowland knew how warm such a chamois skin is! And so we all lie there, each in his hollow, as if the earth has swallowed us up, in heavenly quiet. And then the first foretaste of peace, yes taste, Godchild. That was when we dug up fresh dandelion in a clearing, as you know, Parents, the first and finest salad of the year. In an instant we had all put down our weapons—no, not quite all, one still kept watch—thrown ourselves on our stomachs, dozens of fighters, the clearing full of men on their stomachs, digging out the dandelion shoots with their roots, a couple with pocketknives, most just with their soup spoon, one like this'—he shows it round—'which each one of us has been carrying since the beginning of the war—an essential part of our equipment! Pail after pail full of the fresh dandelion. And how we then stuffed it down. Nothing has ever tasted better, people. And nothing will ever taste better again. "And just like the food now, that's how the peace will be!" one of us said, and after that everyone, everyone. And right away after that we were making plans for peacetime, all at once each of us had one. To be cook, carpenter, furrier, boat-builder, swimming teacher, coffin-maker, wooden-toy carver. One even came up with "politician". But most spontaneously said "dandelion-picker", for the time being at least. And then that night we lit bonfires everywhere on the Svinjska planina, above the treeline—' And for the third time he turns and bends down to me: 'Now make a note of all of that, even if what you've heard goes against the grain for you! —And on all the mountains of our land, on Petzen Peak, on Obir, on Koschuta, on Mittagskogel, on Dobratsch, on Gerlitzen Alp, on Mount Ursula, other bonfires flared up and let the peoples below know, that after the years of the most evil tyranny in human history, the day of liberation of our peoples living here is at hand, and to me it was as if, no, we were certain that the fires could not only be seen here above this land but also on the whole continent and even beyond the oceans, as far as Alaska, Tierra del Fuego and Sumatra. It was no little land, is no little land! And do you know what we did the following morning? Those of us who had already learnt how to dance before the war taught those of us to dance who had been too young then and know about nothing except the forest and the resistance, so that when peace comes, every one of us can dance! Oh, and I forgot to say—write it down, Godson, word for word!—that a miracle happened to me in the dandelion clearing. While feasting there my blind eye became healthy again. For some moments I saw with two eyes what no two-eyed person has ever seen. My dead eye, it lives—there!' Whereupon the father and/or the mother: 'And have you heard anything of your sisters?' And Gregor-Jonatan, a couple of seconds later: 'One sister is still looking for the father of her child out in the Reich, where the bombs are falling. The bastard will be easily scared there. Scared and fatherless. But fatherless— just as well. Perhaps the best thing for him.' Whereupon I try to intervene for once, with dream-heavy tongue. 'Scared doesn't mean timid.' One way or another, no one of my family heard me, because my grandparents go on asking questions: 'And the other? And Ursula? And Snežena?' Jonatan: 'Captured. Incarcerated. In the town. With several others in a death cell.' The father and/or the mother again, after a couple of seconds: 'Why don't you free her?' Jonatan: 'Only the bombs can rescue her. The hum of the Western low-flying aircraft, the only hope, music to the ears of the prisoners. Bomb, bomber, bomb! Do you know why the Nordic race thought it could win the war? Because the bullets would fly past their pointed heads, whereas their enemies with their round heads . . . See you soon, people! Salâm aleïkum! Peace be with you! Pax Christi!' And already he's disappeared.

And once again time passes on the Jaunfeld heath, round my grandparents and me at the roots of the tree. And, then, it's not only as if I am carried away but also the couple on the bench beside me and the boat and the handcart with them. That's perhaps because of the storm now, but which is only blowing in the furthest background, quietly, almost without a sound, whereas we are encamped in calm. In this background—only I see it—there is a different light than at the front where we are, a clear sharp light such as only in spring or early spring. Figures repeatedly appear there, perceived only as mere silhouettes? Shadowy outlines? No, they are too physically present for that, and what will have happened there is also too solid. So I caught sight of a postman, on his bike, cycling along with no hands and whistling as he does so, the wind with or against him, whatever, and unexpectedly, as if struck by lightning, he falls from the bicycle, rolls to the side and remains lying there, while the letters from the postbag whizz through the air. A—do I see rightly?—spring mushroom-picker, his basket full of dark morels and pale St George's mushrooms, collapses just as abruptly and the mushrooms tumble and roll away from the motionless figure. The same thing happens to the ladder man seen earlier, who seems to be on his way back, against the storm—then he crashes to the ground with his ladder, and the same thing with the pair of chimney sweeps, the same with the trio of anglers. A gunshot? None. A woman with a tub of water on her head—the same. A woman with a packet of nappies—the same. A couple with a white cloth, clear in the storm, on a long hazelnut stick—the same. They all tumble together, as if the ground was being pulled away from under their feet. A couple, rolling and pulling an evidently freshly cast church bell—the same. A hecatomb of freshly fallen figures will soon have stiffly lain there. In addition, they were then joined by the ball-carrier, the card-dealer, the holiday-walker and so on; a cook weighed down by potatoes, onions, bottles of wine; a priest in feast-day vestments on his way with a shiny golden monstrance, under a canopy, borne by four altar boys. Finally, or also in the middle of it all, a figure with a giant swastika flag crosses the background. Does the figure swing the flag? It only seems like it, in the storm. In truth, wherever the figure walks and stands, it's cutting the swastika out of the cloth with a large pair of scissors. The storm gusts through the hole, making the remaining white of the flag flutter heavenwards. And what's happening to the flag bearer? Nothing, nothing at all. He parades at length, taking a zigzag course there in the background, back and forth between all the falling or fallen figures and in the end struts off scot-free, also untouched by the stones, or whatever it is, which fall towards him from all skies at the back, and the bird feathers which flutter after them, then whole wings, whole bodies of birds, then animal skulls, animal bodies, which follow.

Has time passed again? Storm still. And now someone is fighting his way against it to the three of us in the calm foreground. Is it him? Yes, it's Gregor, resistance name 'Jonatan', and he's carrying someone in his arms. Is it her? Yes, it's Ursula, resistance name 'Snežena', the snowy one, his sister. And she's no longer alive. Or she's still alive, a moment long, or is that deceptive? stands, sinks down, sits, lies down, dies. Her parents, my grandparents, gradually come to. And from both of them: 'I knew it.' And then from the father or from the mother: 'When did it happen?' Jonatan: 'Only a short time ago. I came too late. She did not turn her gaze away from the torturers. And so the torturers killed her—had to kill her.'

Storm past. Bright light everywhere on our Jaunfeld, as cast only by the May sun. A dove flutters by, and, even if it seems to me to be rather a papery dove, it's a dove. A huge banner floats down out of the sky and dances over the living and the dead: PEACE— FRIEDEN—MIR—SHALOM—SALAM. A thousand birds sing, including the nightingale in broad daylight. The father jumps to his feet, pulls up the apple tree by the roots, as I'm lying there, throws it into nothingness, sits back down on the bench and hits it with his fist and hits it and hits it until the mother places her hand in the crook of his arm and says: 'I know.' Thereupon he takes his daughter from his son, beds her in the boat and pulls it out of my field of vision. The mother stands up from the bench and calls, as if her son is far away: 'Jonatan!' The latter: 'No Jonatan any more, Mother. The fight is over . . . We have . . . won . . . I am Gregor again. Only Snežena will remain Snežena, for ever.' The mother: 'Did she say anything at the end?' Gregor: 'Yes. Our father couldn't stand the word love. "In my house no love." "V moji hiši ni ljubezni. But I love you all. Ampak jaz vas vse ljubim." ' They go home, or wherever, with the handcart, Gregor with his hand on his mother's shoulder as if he's supporting himself.

five

I, the descendant, alone on the bench in the middle of the Jaunfeld, without the tree; in a light which belongs to no season, without a breath of air. Beside me on the bench a kind of kitbag, similar to the one with which one of my mother's brothers once came home on leave during the war. I will have taken a stack of books out of the bag and opened them one after the other. Underlining, taking notes, in between staring into space. As I do so another transformation occurs. Everything remains in its place, however, except that the light turns into that of a long past or not past at all day in May, and a May breeze blows round me and not me alone. And the ringing of bells sets in again on every side, even if from far away. If sirens were to be heard as well, then to sound the all clear. It's Gregor, the survivor of my mother's three brothers, who then approaches. He is no longer in his partisan-or-something uniform but in his best clothes, as once in peacetime. He appears to move a little awkwardly in them, and he still needs a weapon, which is quite small, however, or is it in any case only an air rifle. And when he throws the weapon, or whatever it is, to me, I don't catch it, instead evade it—don't touch it—push it away from me. Unnoticed, he has then blown into an empty paper bag and burst it by my ears, whereupon I gave quite a start. After that he puts a matchbox between his lips and blows through the empty container, like a dart through a blow-pipe, at my head, whereupon I duck. 'Zdravo. Dober dan,' he says then. 'Bog s teboj!' I: 'I beg your pardon?' Gregor: 'I knew it. He doesn't understand our language, not a word. You should have stayed in Wilhelmshaven or Osnabrück. Back with you to Reinbek, Wandsbek, Lübeck. God with you!' He sits down, the books between us, pulls out a harmonica and blows into it, plucks a Jew's harp. Then when he talks he rarely turns to me. What he says, comes out of him undirected, as with the sound of the harmonica, with which, in between, he repeatedly blew more or less the same note. 'The eighth of May nineteen hundred and forty-five was the happiest day of my life, and not only for me but for everyone who, in the forests of the Saualpe, of Petzen Peak, of the Karawanks, had won the end of the war for our homeland. At first I missed my uniform. But soon not any more. In particular, it felt strange after the long long time almost always hidden away on the steep paths used by the chamois, to be able to move freely here on my Jaunfeld. I had to get used to the plain again, and to my hands being free and to having no weight on my back. Just to walk along the old tracks across the fields and along the side of the country road, in the sun, in the spring wind, wearing my Sunday best, hanging loosely and flapping and drumming round my legs as I go—I'd like always to walk along like that, from eternity to eternity, amen. There were some of us, you know, who mounted bicycles left lying by the Swabians. But not to get anywhere more quickly—after all the years in the mountains, they merely wanted to try out cycling, simply spent half the day cycling back and forward on the road, turned round after every small hill and freewheeled back down. There were shouts of joy and sobs and shrieks of delight right across the Jaunfeld, Rosental Valley and Gailtal Valley—less perhaps across the towns, less in Völkermarkt, still less in Klagenfurt, and still less in Friesach and even less than that perhaps in Spittal an der Drau—sobs and shouts of joy and shrieks of delight as then at the end of the day on coming home to their families—if any of them were left and if a home was still there. The eighth of May nineteen forty-five, that was the day I realized how beautiful it is, this Jaunfeld, together with the finest of all scents, the scent of linden blossoms—how beautiful it really and truly is, naša lepa Koroška, our beautiful Carinthia. Beautiful? Beautiful in a different way. What did someone once say? "The beautiful is so hard to see." Yes, until then I had found it hard to see here in our land— or had not seen it all. But on that day I saw the beauty, here, and crystal clear, with one, my only big eye, all day and the day after and the days after that. Simply that the names of the houses were the old ones again, no longer the secret names from the war. No longer "Aware Farm", as the description of our property, but what it had always been, Bleier Farm—Leadworker Farm. The name of our house had never meant anything to me—but now I find it beautiful. And all the other house and farm names that have returned sound to my ears like the returning church bells at the celebration of the Resurrection at Easter—and in the time between, after the death of Jesus on the Cross, there was in their place only the noise of the Good Friday rattles to be heard. This time between, it's over, and of the returned house names I also find those beautiful which we used to mock. "Beim Schoisswohl—Shitewell Farm", "Beim Faulhaber—Idler Farm", "Beim Pruntzer—Pee Farm", "Beim Wixer—Wancker Farm", "Beim Knozer—Stingy Farm", "Beim Wanzerl—Bug Farm", "Beim Figger—Ficking Farm", "Beim Zottel—Shaggy Farm", "Beim Rauber—Robbers Farm", "Beim Tscherfler—Shuffle Farm", "Beim Trentscher—Slobber Farm", "Beim Tschentscher—Grumble Farm", "Beim Eierer—Ballsy Farm", "Beim

Schlecker—Licker Farm", "Beim Kropf—Goitre Farm", "Beim
Hungerleitner—Starveling Farm"—all at once they sound just as
beautiful as Valparaiso, Rijeka, Nižninovgorod, Savannah/Georgia.
Ah, infinitely more beautiful! Ah, altogether today the beauty of
the Jaunfeld place and field names, no matter which, whether of
one syllable or more, whether German or Slovenian, whether Aich
or Dob, whether Lipa or Lind, whether Pliberk or Bleiburg, whether
Saualpe or Svinjska planina, whether Diex or Djekše, whether
Altendorf or Stara vas, whether Gallizien or Galicija. And every
round little hill and every hollow boasts its own name, instead of
"Hill Number Two" or "Position D". How beautiful that is. And
then the landscape itself, the green of the meadows, without fugitives and pursuers, the brown of the forests, without gun flashes
and splintered bark, the blue of the sky, without bombers, and
above all, the white of my blossoming orchard, without—without—without, nothing but the white blossom. And the Drau no
longer our enemy but truly the still river.' He has fallen into a kind
of seated dance. 'And the southern mountains—no Wolf's Lairs or
Winter Fortresses any more, but part of the peacetime land. And
the rhythm of the streams against the pebbles on the bottom the
opposite of a beating of drums. And the gleaming-flickering on the
stream beds here. And on the beds of the streams, where they flow
more slowly, the shadow of the water skaters above. And on the
beds of the streams, where they flow more quickly, the shadows of
the falling leaves whirling past with the pebbles rolling along at
the bottom. And so many pairs of birds in the sky. And the mountain huts nothing but mountain huts, with bacon and bread in the
basket for a snack, a white cloth spread over it, and the jug of must
beside it. And the hayrick stands here will be nothing but hayrick
stands. And the loft nothing but the loft. And the wayside shrines

nothing but wayside shrines. And the flower in bloom beside it, a lady's slipper. Today is the first day of peace here in the land, and that's how it shows itself to us, Godchild. And shows and shows— shows that no one will want us away from here any more, that those forcibly resettled elsewhere will return to their homeland, that on the train, in the bus, in government offices no one will any longer have the nerve to cut us short because of our language. In the name of the oppressed in this land, we have taken our rights into our own hands, taking our cue from the motto of the peasants' revolt of seventeen hundred and thirteen over in Tolmin, in Slovenia: "The Emperor is merely our servant, we shall take things in hand ourselves"—and today is the day on which we have finally, finally won that right. Spet gre za staro pravdo, it's a question of the old right once again. And since eighth May nineteen hundred and forty-five no power can dispute this, our right. From today we are a power—we, who never wanted to have anything to do with power, who did not even have a local or native word for it. From today it is natural for us to embody power, for the first time in our history. And in the preceding days I have even wanted it, power, I!—strange. And strange again, that today on the first day of peace, so it appears to me here in this land, republic and kingdom coincide! All power was with the people, at last, and at the same time our legendary King Matjaž with his host has marched out of the caves of Petzen Peak and into the land after a sleep of a thousand years. Our language, our power. Beyond the language, violence and power breaks out. Supreme power kills the language and, with it, the individual, you and me. To remain in the language. To insist on it! Language, mine, ours—chicken ladder turns into Jacob's ladder. Air—morning air—Easter air—Jaunfeld air! That is the progression.'

The ringing of bells on all sides has long ago faded away. And now the May breezes are abating, too. Spring no longer wafts its ribbon or whatever through the air. I have risen from the bench and, while Gregor was still speaking, have been walking in circles on the heath. Then I approach him, like a messenger, or herald: 'It all lasted less than two weeks. You scented May morning air for exactly ten days. Saw no blood any more, but life. Peace! Then the good peace turned into a bad one and you once again the unsuspecting. It had been planned that way long long beforehand. For ten whole days the warm warm peace and then the cold cold war—which went on and on. The Cold War, it came into force, decreed from the West, from where, here on the Jaunfeld, the cold winds always blow. The British, only just your allies, sometimes more, sometimes less, in your language and freedom struggle, took the stage from one day to the next as your enemies. Your power is over and done with. They are the rulers, the land has been allocated to them, and your Slav brothers in the East let it happen. Your language is once again regarded with hostility, and your local enemies, who always wanted to get rid of it and you, are now hand in glove with the occupiers who not only ban your weapons but also your language.' Gregor: 'All at once they are the knights of the free world and we, only just the freedom fighters with them, are now the dragon to be slain. And who are their squires? Those whom, together, we had just been fighting—the brood of the thousand years. Yesterday, on the way home at night, I was talking to a couple of friends, and suddenly stones were thrown at us and we were shouted at, "dount spik yugoslav!" "This is Ostria!" And none of the new occupiers speaks our language, and when we are summoned to their offices we have to communicate through interpreters and all of them were in the war together with the previous occupiers, on this side and the other side of the Karawanks, were our deadly enemies, from our own folk. And do you know what happens to one of our people, if he contravenes the new ban on assembly? He is locked up in a cell with the White Guards who have fled from Yugoslavia, who killed with BenMu, and with the Heimwehr here and the Ustasha, who murdered for AdHi. And do you know what I feel inside at that? I think about our dead on the Saualpe, on Petzen Peak, at Kömmel Pass, on Koschuta, on the Sattnitz Hills, and I wish I were with them, dead, among my dead, my people. And I tremble, and tremble. And the British greeting, that now means "showing the new occupiers your arse"!' Then I as messenger, though I increasingly stumble over my words: 'Those who had been forcibly resettled, they wanted to send back to the German camps on their return. First they were interned in their own land for a time. When they were at last allowed back to their desolate fields and their farmhouses that had been stripped by looters, they were compelled, if they had managed to raise a few chickens at least, to hand over a portion of the eggs. And if you want to celebrate your old festivals again and perform your old plays again, then you'd better prepare yourselves—they're going to be disrupted. They'll try to stop your festivals and plays.' Gregor: 'Yes, ten days after the end of the war, a "they", a nameless "they", took the place of the earlier supplanters and turned the fresh peace into a rotten one. In the middle of a dance—the only invitation had been to all the world, to dance with us!—a masked "them" storms the hall and throws apples and pears onto the dance floor, not rotten ones, no, the best local produce—and we? We go on dancing, just don't ask me what dance it was!' I: 'The "World Weary Waltz"?' Gregor: ' "The Driving Out the Devil Polka". "The Go to Hell Kolo". Or, if you like, the square dance which dances away evil, as in your Western. For a while it was part of our dance to pick up the apples and pears and bite into them. But then . . . the fight, the broken bones, an eye knocked out. And don't ask me what the competent peacetime judge will then have decided.' He quotes: ' "The injuries do not fall within the sphere of the dispensation of justice, since at fairs and public dances it has been from time immemorial, as everywhere in Austria, the custom that those in attendance come to blows." And in the middle of our theatre performances, which have been taken up again, windowpanes shattering and stones crashing onto the stage, and out of the darkness the bellowing: "Away with the bandit language, away with you. The stage free for the original language, the language of the country, the only language here!" We finish the play nevertheless, don't ask me how. These stone-throwers are masked. In the war I was masked for a time myself. But I don't ever want to see masks again. There are no peaceful masks. And don't ask me now what happened to me and the other fighters at the last Sunday Mass.' I: 'I know. You went to the Communion rail—' Gregor: '—and as we knelt there to receive the body of the Lord, after which we had so hungered during the years in the forest, this Communion was an incomparable need for us all, as was, on the other hand, the need to lie with a woman, a need? A homesickness!, then—' I: '—then the priest ignored you as you were kneeling there! just like that!' Gregor: '—and has given the body of Christ to those others kneeling and I and our people were kneeling for a long time with outstretched tongues ready to receive, before I understood—no, I understood nothing and will never understand it. Those who have just proclaimed in the Gospel "Life has been made manifest!" have made that life disappear again, for ever and ever, by refusing Communion.' I as messenger or reporter: 'Many of the priests in the land are new. In the war, they took part in the violence of the foreign tyrants beyond the mountains, and, after their flight, were appointed to the same posts here as on the other side, while many of your local pastors, teachers, lawyers and doctors left you to yourselves and settled in the new Yugoslavia.' Gregor: 'The new Yugoslavia as the only possibility—to my sorrow, to my disappointment! Because here is where I belong, and it is to here that I'm always drawn back, only here have I been happy, if ever. My heart is in the Jaunfeld. The new Yugoslavia is no more than the last resort, is it that? No, because if I left the Jaunfeld, our property, our estate, our farm would be gone. Not a few of us are now sitting by the mild Adriatic Sea, in Koper, in beautiful Piran, in Portorož, in Ankaran and—are homesick for the forests and the snow here, all of it! Are in need, need of being here—just as my brother Benjamin once wrote from up in the tundra: "Every soul longs to travel home." Our eternal Jaunfeld homesickness—how sick I am of it, this domotožje. And yet we never get rid of it, never ever. Because here we are at home, not beyond the Karawanks, not in Slovenia, not in Yugoslavia, not by the Adriatic, not in Piran. Here, here is where we are at home, on the Jaunfeld, between Saualpe and Petzen Peak, in our Carinthia, v naši Koroški. On the other hand— our farm, it's anyway half-dead. My sister in a foreign land and the foreign land is burnt to the ground. And in the house a silent looking away, all the livelong day. Even in the cow and pigsheds our language is no longer heard out loud, and without caraway and vinegar no sauerkraut.' I: 'And the very latest . . .' Gregor: 'Play the messenger.' I: 'The bearer of bad tidings, too?' Gregor: 'Play him.' I: 'The new power has burnt your orchard, the one from before the war—they need space to park their tanks.' Gregor: 'They were still young, my trees.' I: 'They cried out in the fire, the pear and apple trees, the trunks so full of juice, and then when they burst it sounded like fireworks—' Gregor: '—which we used to set off on Easter night to celebrate the Resurrection.'

For a while both of us were silent and lost in thought as we walked round and round the bench in the middle of the Jaunfeld. Then Gregor spoke: 'Now it's quite dead, our farm. I'm finally deprived of power—we are. Powerless. And the example of our orchard makes me realize just how much power I did have. Our last bit of power. But what a power. What a loss, the loss of that power. Powerless, helpless. The Germans, in the war, burnt down our houses and barns, but at least they left us our fruit trees. And now the liberators from the West, the Tommies and the Charlies, the Limies and the Georges, they're finishing us off. And that from a country, from which some of the most beautiful fruits come, the most noble, the tastiest. Help us, Mister or Sir Cox, you who have blessed us with the apple Cox's Orange. Fruit-farmer, *sadjar*, William, to whom we owe the William's Pear, the one with the tender yellow-white flesh, stand by us. Another gardener, Thomas, you who gave us *Far From the Madding Crowd* and your name to the Beurre Hardy Pear, stand by us. Grower, over there, on the other side of the Channel, of the Lemon Yellow Cousin, *žlahtnik*, with its scent of wine, intercede for us. Father of the London Adam's Rib, intercede for us. But you who are here now, from the other side of the Channel, who behave here worse than you ever did in your colonies, sweetie- and chocolate-throwers by day, flame-throwers by night: May your teeth fall out, you successor-ragged devils. May your Wolverhampton Wanderers wander down into the County League, and stay at the bottom until the twelfth of never. May the Tottenham Hotspurs be shot down in cold blood and disappear without trace. May Manchester United dissolve into particles of dust. May your West Bromwich Albion blow game after game. The old names have returned. Yes! But they don't say anything any more, they don't mean anything any more . . .'

Meanwhile we have both continued walking in a circle, each in his own. And now I once again approach my godfather as messenger, with a badly acted radio announcer's voice, increasingly stumbling over my words—mixing them up—stuttering: 'And again I know something that you don't know. And again I have to be the bearer of bad tidings, of one calamity and then another. But perhaps it is not a calamity at all, but rather the run of events, the course of history? The first: the excommunication in the year nineteen forty-eight, pronounced by Moscow against the new Yugoslavia. And you here, the former forest soldiers, what consequences will it have for you, in the land which, together with what has happened so far, you continue to see as your land?' Gregor: 'The only ones in the New Austria who appeared as our allies, even if only half-heartedly, after all during the war they had already avoided fighting side by side with us, the Moscow listeners, they will, in the twinkling of an eye, include us in the excommunication of the New Yugoslavia. In the twinkling of an eye we are a people without representatives—we, the victors. Those who before then have represented us after a fashion, but at least that, in the distant capital will not only turn away from us but will also fight us to the point of denying us existence. Are we as a result finally alone in the land of our birth and childhood? To whom can we turn now?' I have meanwhile continued walking in a circle and once again come closer as the messenger who stumbles over, mixes up his words . . . : 'Another year has passed, and in Paris, outside the city, the foreign ministers of the Soviet Union, the United States, Great

Britain and France have decided in secret negotiations, that the territory of your people is to remain part of the state of Austria—'
Gregor: '—which treats us as not deserving the title a "people".
And that is the reward we get for being the only ones to fight,
some, then many, then very many of us, for the liberation of the
country, as was the condition of the Declaration of nineteen forty-
three—again Moscow—that Austria be allowed to call itself independent again after the war. A country that doesn't want us, and
that is allowed to stand there again as a state, right in the middle
of the continent, thanks to us. Course of history? Not rather a
dragon biting its tail? And not hurting itself at all in doing so?' I
have meanwhile walked in my circle and approach yet again playing the part of messenger or amateurish radio announcer: 'And
meanwhile years have passed again and the country is free. The
foreign troops will withdraw. The red-white-red book, at the very
beginning of which Austria cites the fight of the Slovenians of
Carinthia as proof of its liberation struggle in the Second World
War—it has done its duty.' Gregor: 'And now we can go, finally. Or
fall silent, from census to census, from bus journey to bus journey,
from tavern evening to tavern evening. A comfort that, to be the
heroes in the red-white-red book? If you ask me . . . But no one
will ever ask me here. How I have always resisted any notions of
the tragic. Tragedies in Ancient Greece, if you like, or for the American Indians—but not here, with us! Even the word itself is a foreign word in our language, and not only in my father's house. From
farm to farm, from field to field, from wayside shrine to wayside
shrine, from mountaintop to mountaintop—no mention of it. But
this now . . . It cries out, shrieks, whimpers, trembles for the word
"tragedy"—against my will, against our nature, against my heart.
Have mercy on us! But that's what I should have said at the begin-

ning of the Mass. And it must be over by now, only the blessing is still to be given . . . Ah, blessing . . . Only a miracle can set things right for us. But in history there are no miracles, are there? Sometimes I wish the earlier tyranny back. The devils of those days at least knew they were devils. The devils of today, on the other hand, pretend they are angels and are devilish without end and are devilish in the morning, devilish in the evening, devilish at night . . . And that's the whole story . . .'

Finally he has sat down on the bench, which has visibly—or does it just appear so to me?—sunk down into the Jaunfeld soil. For a long time we were both silent. Then Gregor, turning to me: ' "No big tragedy," you'll say. "The main thing is, one's still alive." But who is one? And what's life? History, it's eaten up my life and our life, the feeling of being alive. And what's life, if one doesn't feel alive? Yes, it's a tragedy, one that's a good laugh.' (He 'laughs') 'And, apart from that, it's a tragedy for which we fighters in the forests are partly to blame. Our triumph, wasn't it this, to have grasped the course of history at the right moment? And how did it go on—one can only laugh.' (He 'laughs') 'For centuries the slaves of history, we imagined, we had become its masters at last, and that's precisely how we turned ourselves into its victims. Is it not said that part of a tragedy is the presumption of the one struck by it? Were we forest fighters not presumptuous, when we appropriated our right? Presumptuous how? In relation to whom or what? In relation to God and the gods? In relation to the starry sky? In relation to the self-denial of our forebears? "Anything, but just no politics! Politics as compulsion—instead of keeping house sensibly!"? As for me, Swinetz Gregor—not even the old spelling has been revived in the land! Never, even with a weapon in the mountains, did it occur to me that I was making history. I never dreamt of it. Not even with my face painted would I want to see myself as a maker of history. In any case, ever since I was little, I just wanted things always to remain as they are—for nothing to change, summer and winter, house and farm, sun and snow, wind and windlessness. If I still have any wish at all—then, to be in the presence of my apples and my pears. Only it's all over with them long ago, it doesn't pay anyway. The apple is still called Cox's Orange, but its other name at the markets is "allergy apple", and the Anjou Pear comes from the United States and the Kaiser Alexander Pear from Italy. And a second wish—to play skittles with my father and my brothers and the last of the skittles doesn't fall and doesn't fall and we're all shouting and shouting "Fall over, bastard!" A modest wish, isn't it? Yes, as far as Swinetz Gregor is concerned, he knows he doesn't share the blame for the course of history. But not a few of his fellow fighters from the forests feel they are to blame. Would they otherwise keep silent right up to the present day about what we did? They don't even open their mouths in front of their children and grandchildren. And let it happen when the brood of the brood of the thousand years, calls them "bandits", just as the brood once did. Ah, you imperishable brood, seem to be the only imperishable thing in this God's world. Ah, I could throw the Jonatan Apple up in the air like so, as I did yesterday, as I did as a child. Ah, out of the nightmare of history at last, and nothing but eternal childhood. Unhappy the people, is it not so, that becomes a people of history—turned from a victim people into an active and victorious one, it forces another people into the role of the victim people, does it not? Unhappy the unconquered!? Should we have gone on being the silent sufferers? Have gone on allowing the language of our soul to be taken away from us? Through our struggle did we not earn our homeland? And what about now? Ach, history. Oh, life. Learning from history? Yes, hopelessness. What do you want from us, Descendant? Why us? We lost after all. Aren't a subject. And also no stuff that dreams are made on. Search out some other material, something contemporary. The Mariazell cable car disaster, for example, the football war on Heldenplatz in Vienna, the illegitimate children of the Pope.'

I will then have crouched beside him on the half-sunken bench in the middle of the Jaunfeld, asking the question: 'But can history not also be a form, and form means peace?' Gregor: 'Next you'll be trying to tell me about the soul of the world. Soul of the world— solid rubber. And the soul of the individual—lice-ridden.' There then developed a kind of statement-response competition between me and my godfather, of a kind that I remember from the area we come from. I: 'False, the world now? Don't you know the method of the Balkan musicians? If they happen to play a false note, then they play on with it to make a new tune? Look, the birds over the Jaunfeld. Each one flies differently, differently high, differently fast, and each one flies now, and now.' Gregor: 'The birds, where? And this now—' Is he not imitating his dead brother? '—I wasn't born yesterday!' Thereupon I: 'And listen—the ringing of bells throughout the whole of Carinthia, from Villach to Ferlach right up to Gurk—' Thereupon Gregor: 'What bells? I don't hear any-thing—' (there really is nothing to be heard) '—not from Villach or Ferlach or Gurk.' (Did he not speak in his father's voice?) There-upon I: 'But the wind, which unites the peoples in the land, which ignores borders—you do hear that, don't you?' Gregor listens in all directions of the compass, where again there will be nothing to be heard: 'You and your other time. It's over and done with—when will you finally admit it?' Thereupon I: 'But did your mother not always say: "God loves to return"?' And he: 'You and your delusion of peace.' Thereupon I: 'But that space—does it not still remain open?' He: 'The war drove that out of me, too. It only bore fruit, as long as I was child of love.' Thereupon I: 'To lie here on the bench, Forebear, with a woman, under the starry sky—is that nothing?' He against that: 'No woman ever lay with me. A one-eyed man and a woman, that doesn't make a couple, not even under the starry sky. A woman and a blind man, that's more likely.' Thereupon I: 'Here, you are child of *my* love. You forebears are all children of my love. Not simply that I would like to let a light burn day and night in front of the picture of you all—more than that I would like to stroke your skulls, hold them in my hands, like so! No, to me you are not skulls, but faces! I venerate you. Why? Because you were faint hearts, but brave ones. As if faint hearts and bravery belonged together. And nor were you ever aggressors. Only in defence did you become men, and become women, and what men and women! Let another eternal light shine for you! That's how I think of you, and, the other way round, think myself thought by you. I want to trace your hands, your eyes, the way you place your feet. Hear your voices, in the middle of my heart, in the middle of a dream and outwith the dream. Strange that the outline of those deceased is so much stronger and lasting than that of those alive today. There will never be your like again. No day without you. And without you no morning. With you I come to my senses. You are my good sense, you are what determines me. Thanks to you I shall always uphold the Jaunfeld here and with it the land between the Karawanks and the Svinjska planina—thanks to you, through you, in you and with you! I consent to my own dying. But not to yours, Forebears, not and not again, forever not.

And I would forever want to apologize to you because I am living.
You should stand up from the dead. I call you to rise out of the
graves from the dead. May God honour your faces.' Thereupon he,
after a longer silence: 'A child of love, that is you yourself, Descendant. Only a child of love paints with such naive brushstrokes. Put
together out of his dreamt-up and dreamt-away worlds. Dreams,
and decides that we dead are not dead. Dead we are, Descendant,
dead. Dead night after night and without a Day of Judgement.
Nothing more incomprehensible than a child of love.' Thereupon
I: 'Heaven is satisfied with a tree with a single flower.' Thereupon
he: 'Sooner or later everyone turns into a ghost.' Thereupon I: 'A
children's swing is spinning round over there.' Thereupon he: 'And
the second rope has torn and the seat is hanging upside down.'
Thereupon I (gradually our words are beginning to turn into song):
'At last storm clouds.' He: 'The singer sings until he falls silent.' I:
'The tail of the lizard by the side of the track points to the horizon.'
He: 'Are those swallows flying there or midges?' I: 'There's a storm
blowing on the Packsattel Pass, and on the early morning Graz–
Klagenfurt bus children were thrown against the windows, which
shattered.' He: 'The murderer's confession calls on the victim in
the grave to stand up from the dead. All my life I walked in show-
ers of ash, with garments full of holes, from island to island. He
who is dying is the spy from the other world. What do you know,
a fatherless child?' I: 'The fatherless child knows something else. I
can only recommend fatherlessness. The knight of knights, for
example, was fatherless: Parsifal.' He: 'And dear little Jesus . . .
Oh, all the stories about our struggle for life and survival, about
our language struggle, about our struggle for our Slovenščina, for
the words of our language, za besede našega jezika, for the words
of our soul, za besede naše duše, all the stories that concern every-

one—read by whom? Oh, all the books about us mountain goats on the avalanche, about us little people on a grand highway. Oh, Karel Prušnik, oh, Lipej Kolenik, oh, Tone Jelen, oh, Anton Hader-lap, oh, Helene Kuchar-Jelka . . . And then you fatherless child, with your fatherless Parsifal. Oh! Oh! and once again oh!'

At that I admit defeat. My forebear has stood up from the bench and left me sitting there alone. And he doesn't seem to be finished yet with me or whoever. Because all at once he turns into rage incarnate, at the same time a rage so gentle and helpless, such as I have never experienced before: 'I have become a misanthropist. I would never have dreamt it, I, who once, in those days, before the war, had a good word to say about everyone, and who once felt pity for all, even the murderers. And I so object to having become a misanthropist, a mankind-hater! I know that my misanthropy is wrong. And yet I've had enough of people and every day imagine myself going for them, for him, for him, for her, and her—and liq-uidating them. Yet no one is doing anything to me—not any more. Even those who once caused havoc among our people, as if they were the very devil, now in old age express their regret to me. 'I did great wrong. I am not an honourable person. It's true, I did nothing to harm your father when he cursed the great German Reich in public—he had his youngest son and the latter's ultimate sacrifice to thank for that, not me. It's true, I turned a blind eye when your mother watered down the milk. But I nevertheless wronged you badly. It's true, when I had to take your partisan sister prisoner I only aimed the warning shot at her legs. It's true, I con-gratulated your second sister on the birth of her child. Even expressed my respect to her for her going against the family grain and choosing as father of the child a man from the nation foreign to her. In addition, I brought a bouquet of winter roses to the mother and newborn. But the fact remains—I wronged you very badly indeed. I am not an honourable person. And no one can take my guilt from me. I have to live and live, and live with my wrong-doing.' (Again in his own voice.) 'Ah, there was a time, when I got rid of these people by mimicking them. Such a casting out of devils today—without any effect. The Devil is in me, a thousand devils are in me. Another of these dictators on TV, see how he struts about—' He imitates one, arms swinging, held away from the body. 'I can't get rid of any of them, they're part of me. The disgust, ("that's 'isgusting") of our dead Benjamin at the milk skin on his coffee, at the maggots in the cheese, at all the rubber bands lying there in a figure eight, at noodles in the form of an *S*, it seems to have got into me as disgust, as disgust at people today, now. There was a time when I sang away my disgust at the present, no, no hymns—by singing the songs of our land here. Yes, in the songs I could hear the sound of your time, the other time.' He really did sing that, and immediately broke off again: 'Doesn't work. Now the singing makes the disgust twice as strong. At best the sounds of our clan, as they slip out of me in fright—' He utters the sound 'in pain—' He utters the sound 'and simply in aversion—' He utters the sound 'they alone help me out of my disgust, for moments at a time—above all our very own Jaunfeld sigh, against all the German borderland songs . . .' (He gives a sigh for me, I sigh in imitation of him, we sigh in chorus and, round us, invisibly, the sighing cho-rus swells up and breaks off abruptly.) 'There was a time when I fought my disgust. But now the fight is over. The disgust has won. I, a misanthropist? Worse, a despiser of mankind. All these regular partings, even in the hair of small children—what's happened to the beautiful irregular ones? I know, when it comes to people there are all kinds. But why do I meanwhile meet only the other kind? Refined people! Oh, I am so in need of them. How I . . . long . . . for them. But I only encounter people acting refined. And kind people, how they are needed. Instead, at most, now and then a good soul. A kind person is something else! Or at least a bad person, whom I could offer new resistance.' I: 'The people disappear, and the t-shirts fade.' He: 'Instead—only the unkind and ungood. The ungood are always and everywhere, and cannot be fought.' I: 'Most beautiful of all are the wild plum trees at the barn door that keep it shut.' He: 'Ah, you people today have so much more time than we had and get up to so much more nonsense.' I: 'The snake there at the edge of the field is playing Vision.' He: 'There was a time when I constantly used to have hot hands, and now they're always cold.' I: 'The shirts tear in the icy water.' He: 'I can pull myself up by my own bootlaces as often as I like—I don't get anywhere.' I: 'The blackbird and the robin redbreast are singing.' He: 'I am disgusted by birds, too, by the blackbird's yellow beak, by the red robin bib.' He gives the bench a kick: 'No prayer has ever been heard, at least not any of mine.' I: 'We sat long enough in the snow.' He: 'One of my weapons I didn't hand over to the British.' I: 'What is it? It's lying under the bench, and if one touches it, it cries out?' He hesitates: 'Tell me, Descendant.' I: 'A chain.' He: 'Where did you get that from?' I: 'An old riddle, from the Jaunfeld.' He: 'From the Jaunfeld. A chain. To harness the horses. Under the bench. If one touches it, it cries out.' I conjure up an apple. He grabs it from my hand and throws it away. We stay where we are. We sigh the clan sigh, together. Then Gregor: 'Because we two are the last, we stand as a shining example to the rest of the world, don't we? And what does the rest of the world do? It goes on being more and more. And now it's *my* turn with a riddle: What cries out *on* the benches, and seizes hold of me against my will, and clatters and bangs, and rages and roars, and thunders and rumbles, that it's just not nice any more?' I: '?' Gregor: 'Humankind.'

And, unexpectedly, it's now Gregor who conjures something up, shows it to me, shows it round, shows it to every side—a Sunday-best dark jacket. I: 'What's that?' Gregor: 'A part of the Sunday-best suit, the only one, of my youngest brother, Benjamin. The jacket has been waiting for you in the wardrobe at home until the time was ripe. Stand up, Descendant.' I stood straight up from the bench half sunk into the Jaunfeld. Gregor: 'Hands out of your pockets, Godchild. Arms out. Chin up!' He puts the jacket on me. But as I slip into it, left then right, it frays instantly, turns to dust, hangs in tatters from my body. And while I remain standing there, arms outspread, I hear from my forebear: 'Jaunfeld. Moths and leeches. Lead and mica. Water skaters and cowdung. Communion cup and chicken ladder . . .' And then I come in: 'May devotions and death knells. Forest bunker and toadstools. Blue work trousers and red resurrection mantles. Lenten veils and swastikas. Clogs and mouse-traps. Rabbits and raspberries. Zajci in maline. Buckwheat and calendars. Ajda in koledar. Beets and rainbows. Repice in mavrice. Sun and snow. Sonce in sneg . . .' And, again unexpectedly, it is then I, assuming the part of an advance guard or even a leader, who with outspread arms, and without turning round, signals to the Jaunfeld background, to make an appearance, to join the two of us.

And as I glance over my shoulder into the emptiness, the whole clan, believe it or not, now appears, one at a time, each one just as he ever was and dressed just right. Simultaneously Gregor: 'No! not like this. You have no right to a fairy tale. And now you're playing the director as well. Once the homeland is lost—the homeland is lost for ever. The storm's still blowing. Continuous storm. Storm still. History—the Devil in us, in me, in you, in all of us, plays God, final arbiter, absolute principle. And the sum of wrongs becomes the sum of right. Yes, we were in the wrong—wrong to be born here, just here.' I: 'Yes, I am the director. It is I who grasps right in his hand for you, the old right. An end to me as dreamer, one who looks on powerless at what and how he dreams. I am awakened. I am power. Jaz sem oblast. Jaz sem avtoriteta. I'm the one who determines . . .' Gregor: 'Into whom are you breathing such life? A dayfly!' I: 'Perhaps. Yes, a dayfly! How beautiful they are, the dayflies, how light, how breezy!'

And then from behind a hand is placed on my shoulder, one so unfamiliar, that I spin round, startled. In front of me stands a young man, who up to that point had presumably been hidden behind my mother. I: 'Who's he? What's he doing here?' My mother: 'It's you. You yourself. As you've grown older has it not been your wish, your great wish to stand facing your earlier self?' I: 'Yes. But myself as a child! A child playing. Learning to read. Looking in wonder. Listening to the wind. Listening into it. Letting himself be sprayed by the rain. Hopping along a field track in the dawn light, holding Grandfather's hand. And not as adolescent prick, as weak-kneed spectacles wearer, as spotty-face.' My mother: 'You can't determine everything, my son.' And so now I take a step backwards, to the side, forward, walk round myself, circle round myself, inspect myself, examine myself, regard myself, shake my head at myself, frown and raise my eyebrows at myself, am moderately surprised at myself, punch myself in the stomach, kick myself in the back of the knee, grab myself by the neck, and then tussle with myself—who is stronger, I or I?—and to end I'm seized by the hair by myself and whirled round.

And so then one of us began to sing, Gregor, I think:

'A grave has been dug for me,
deep and wide
but I was too big for it,
and the grave too small.
And so our whole land
was dug
as a grave for me—'

And another one of us, Valentin, I think, interrupted him by starting to sing his 'We shall gather at the river—' And he in turn is interrupted by Benjamin, or whoever, who breaks in with his 'No milk today—', whereupon he in turn is interrupted by his sister Snežena with the beginning of a partisan song, which in its turn is immediately drowned out by my mother with her God-knows-what tremolo, which always made me want to cover my ears when I was a child . . . but this singer, too, is stopped by the song of my grandfather now, I think:

'I have no father no more,
I have no mother no more,
nor a brother,
nor a sister, nor a friend.
I'm an abandoned child,
like the mountain-meadow wind—'

Then my grandmother breaks in, correcting him or varying the song:

    'like a bush in the wind—'

And then singing together:

    '—I'm Old World-Weary!
    That's what they call me — — —'

And finally this singing couple was also interrupted, by the rest of us all speaking at once: 'Oh, the "*World Weary Waltz*", yet again, never anything but the old "World Weary" . . .' 'And never played as anything but a waltz here . . .' 'And sung as a waltz, always sad . . .' 'And always danced in melancholy three-quarter time . . .' 'Hey, why not for once try "World Weary" as a polka?!' 'Yes: for once play our "World Weary" as a polka!' . . .' 'Once, just once, vary our "World Weary Waltz" as a polka . . .' 'Yes! Away with the waltz past!' 'World Weary POLKA!' . . . 'Not exactly music of the future either, but well . . .'

And already the invisible harmonica has got us in tune, and we sing our centuries-old 'World Weary Waltz' transformed into a polka, more and more at the tops of our voices and with all our might, and hitting especially wrong notes as we sing, I, too, even I.

To be added is, that at some point during our last appearance together—my memory says, perhaps before my grandfather began his 'World Weary'—I intervened once again. By raising my arms I requested my forebears to be silent, and then said (unclear, whether to myself, or out loud): 'Not so long ago I was in a former gold-rush settlement in Alaska. Now it's a place for tourists, packed all day long with visitors from all over the world. Among the crowds a couple of original inhabitants, or natives, in this case American Indians of the Athabasca tribe. They can also be recognized, because they don't move but sit, squat, crouch, and that too on the bare earth, and each of the few survivors by himself, far away from the next, and only from time to time do the few stand up as if at a common sign and briefly wave to one another from a distance over the tourists' heads: Hey, I'm still here!—And me, too!—And me!, and then they squat down again.'

And to be added is also that as I was relating this (whether only in my head or out loud), at my hand-clapping and finger-snapping, all those many came up, on all sides, who had earlier passed by in the background. Now they crowd forward and part us from one another, just like that, as if we didn't exist, so that we for our part gradually find ourselves in the background for our farewell, and as the song comes to an end will have more or less disappeared between and behind the others, recognizable at most by the movement of our hands as we still wave to one another.